A Handbook
of the
Religious Life

A Handbook
of the
Religious Life

For the use of those concerned with the administration
of the Religious Life in the Church of England with
guidelines for those making personal vows

Fifth Edition 2004

Advisory Council on the Relations of
Bishops and Religious Communities

CANTERBURY
PRESS
Norwich

First published in 2004 by Canterbury Press Norwich
(a publishing imprint of Hymns Ancient & Modern Ltd, a registered charity)
St Mary's Works, St Mary's Plain, Norwich,
Norfolk NR3 3BH, United Kingdom

www.scm-canterburypress.co.uk

British Library Cataloguing in Publication data.

A catalogue record for this book is available from the British Library

ISBN 1-85311-618-1

Printed and bound in Great Britain by
The Bidnall Press Ltd, Beccles, Suffolk

CONTENTS

APPENDICES

PREFACE TO THE FIFTH EDITION

The Advisory Council on the Relations of Bishops and Religious Communities (ACRBRC) published its first *Directory* in 1943. Revised editions were published in 1957 and 1976 with the fourth edition of *A Directory of the Religious Life* being published in 1990.

In 1999 the Advisory Council noted that there should be a substantial re-write of the *Directory* as it was out of date and did not take into account the changes taking place to Religious communities. Some communities are noticeably ageing, some are entering into contracts with seculars and other adjustments are being made which bring community members into new relationships with those with whom they work and function. It is therefore vital for communities to be acquainted with current legislation and particularly those laws pertaining to charities, trusteeship, property, employment rights, health and safety and child protection. The *Directory* also had to take account of the growing number of people who were called to live the single consecrated life.

This document has always been known as the *Directory* but in recent times the definition of the word 'directory' has changed. People now associate it solely with books listing subscribers, members of professions, etc. They are not aware that a 'directory' can also contain directions, rules and guidance. Regretfully the Council has had to accept this change and, although the content remains basically the same, it has decided to call this new edition *A Handbook of Religious Life*.

A small sub-group was set up by the Council to undertake a comprehensive review of the *Handbook* and to re-write is as necessary. The Council is most grateful to all the members of the sub-group who worked so hard over a number of years to produce the new *Handbook*. It would also like to thank the members of the Personal Vows sub-group who drew up the guidelines for those living the single consecrated life. The Council also owes a debt of gratitude to Dr Petà Dunstan for the work she has done in editing and indexing the *Handbook* and for writing the most interesting Historical Summary.

The Council is very grateful to the Canterbury Press for agreeing to publish the *Handbook*. It will now stand alongside its sister publication the very successful and enormously helpful *Anglican Religious Communities Year Book*.

It is the wish of the Council that the *Handbook* will serve as a code of practice (valid at the time of publication) to be followed and referred to by Religious communities, bishops, those who wish to set up new communities and those who wish to lead consecrated lives outside a community.

✝Jack Sheffield
Chairman ACRBRC
23 April 2004
George, Martyr, Patron of England

FOREWORD

The Church of England recognises the importance of Religious communities in the Church and values their life and witness, but has no ecclesiastical law to protect and regulate them. The Advisory Council on the Relations of Bishops and Religious Communities was set up in 1935 to express the Church's care for the Religious Life by providing a means of episcopal oversight appropriate to the particular circumstances of the Church of England.

The primary purpose of this *Handbook* (formerly the *Directory*) is the definition and description of the standards that are accepted for these purposes by the bishops in the name of the Church. The *Handbook* is therefore not a legislative code, but a corpus of norms or authoritative standards. Adherence to these norms, like the acceptability of variations from them, is entrusted to the oversight of the Visitors of communities. Each Visitor is the episcopal guarantor to the Church at large of the community's right to the Church's confidence and the community's guide in maintaining that confidence.

Communities with branch houses in other provinces of the Anglican Communion are subject to the laws of those provinces. In those areas where there are no provincial canons or local Handbook or Directory for the ordering of the Religious Life, the communities concerned should negotiate with the provincial and diocesan authorities the extent to which the provisions of this *Handbook* apply to those houses (see also paragraphs **509** and **1002a**).

Although it is clear from its constitution that the Advisory Council on the Relations of Bishops and Religious Communities has responsibility only for matters relating to communities living under vows, the House of Bishops in a resolution of 4 June 1985 expressed its encouragement and concern for other forms of Christian communal life, some of which have existed in the Church of England for half a century or more.

These other styles of community usually have some degree of approval from the diocesan bishop, but are not formally recognised by the Advisory Council or represented in the General Synod of the Church of England; nor are they listed by the Advisory Council as taking part in the election of community representatives to the Council. The Council nevertheless takes an active interest in all approaches to community living, including those that are experimental – not least for the light that such experiences contribute to the understanding and renewal of community life under vows.

Each community is given its own distinctive gifts and call from God for the building up of the whole Church. The provisions of the *Handbook* are intended to help Visitors and communities in ways consonant with the Church's expectations, while preserving the proper freedom of each community to follow Christ under the guidance of the Holy Spirit in accordance with the gifts and call it has received.

If in any instance the norms presented in this *Handbook* are at variance with the provisions of the governing instruments of a community, the governing instruments of the community are to be followed. The community is in such cases advised to consider the revision of its instruments, and is encouraged to report its decision to the Advisory Council.

The Church of England Advisory Council on the Relations of Bishops and Religious Communities

CONSTITUTION

(Ratified by the House of Bishops 23 January 1990)

I   The Advisory Council shall serve the needs of the two provinces of Canterbury and York.

II   Its functions shall be:

(1)   to advise the House of Bishops and individual bishops on matters concerning the relations of bishops and Religious communities;

(2)   to advise diocesan bishops, communities and their visitors on any matters they may refer to the Council;

(3)   to give guidance to those who wish to form communities.

III   The composition of the Advisory Council shall be as follows:

(1)   chairman and convenor, a diocesan bishop appointed by the Archbishops of Canterbury and York;

(2)   three bishops nominated by the House of Bishops;

(3)   ten members elected by the Religious communities.[1] The method of election shall be settled and carried out by the Advisory Council;

(4)   not more than five co-opted members;

(5)   all members shall serve for five years and shall be capable of re-appointment or re-election;

(6)   a secretary may be appointed by the Council.

IV   Decisions of the Council shall be made by a simple majority of members, provided that in any matter of principle, change in constitution or change in the Handbook, that majority shall include the approval of at least three of the bishops appointed by the archbishops and the House of Bishops.

V   Changes in this constitution require ratification by the House of Bishops.

---

[1] All professed, both temporary and life, and others who have voting rights in elections within their own community, are entitled to vote for their representatives on the Advisory Council.

HISTORICAL SUMMARY

The emergence of Religious communities in the mid-Victorian period took the Church of England bishops somewhat by surprise. Within the next fifty years, the number of both Religious and communities increased not only in Great Britain, but in other parts of the Anglican Communion. From South Africa to North America, the Indian sub-continent to the Pacific, matters concerning the Religious Life began to be raised for episcopal judgement. Bishops were asked to adjudicate in arguments over property, clashes over individuals seeking release from vows, and in questions concerning ministries in their dioceses. The relationship between some bishops and some communities became strained, with unresolved disputes continuing for long periods. Finding solutions was sometimes hampered because there were no canons governing these matters. Many bishops, whether sympathetic or not to Religious Life, began to feel the need for some kind of regulation.

From the communities' point of view, their growth and increasing contribution to the Church's ministry and witness entitled them to some formal recognition from the episcopal authorities. They sought an acknowledgement of their role and value, an official sanction and encouragement for their particular call. This, they believed, would afford protection against the (still) powerful voices in the Church, including some on the episcopal bench, who were hostile to Religious Life in principle.

The bishops at the 1897 Lambeth Conference therefore began discussion on the relations of bishops and Religious communities, setting up a committee to produce a report. However the suspicions which had arisen during the Victorian period made agreement difficult. Communities feared episcopal interference in their internal affairs by bishops with unsympathetic views, whilst bishops feared giving a recognition which might be exploited by maverick or undisciplined groups. The report when finally published in 1902 was not acted upon. The 1908 Lambeth Conference returned to the subject, but no resolution was reached before the outbreak of the First World War in 1914 produced more urgent priorities.

In the 1920s, the bishops' committee on Religious communities in Britain took up the issue once again and in 1926 (before any effective consultation with the communities themselves) had printed a set of draft regulations, which then went though several revisions. Alarm began to spread through many communities that regulations were about to be 'imposed', and to quell the fears a meeting was held in Oxford in January 1930. Up to one hundred Anglican Religious met.

They protested particularly about the idea that the diocesan bishop would *de jure* be the Visitor to a community, and insisted the choice of Visitor must be a freedom for every community. The Religious chose representatives from their number to meet with representatives of the bishops on 11 February 1930, with the Warden of Keble College, Oxford, Dr B J Kidd, in the chair. Dr Kidd was a lecturer in theology and knowledgeable on the history and traditions of Religious Life and was seen as an impartial and authoritative facilitator.

Despite much discussion – at the Lambeth Conference of 1930, and further meetings between the representatives of the two sides in January 1931 and again six months later – a compromise failed to emerge. However, from the meeting of 29 June–1 July 1931 came the idea of the committee of joint representatives continuing to meet regularly. If there could not yet be regulations or canons passed by the Church, perhaps there could be an Advisory Council as a temporary measure? This would at least provide a place for concerned bishops or Religious to turn for advice when disputes arose. The advisory committee would be chaired by a diocesan bishop and have representatives from the communities, plus experts on church history and theology appointed by the Archbishops of Canterbury and York.

The suggestion was taken up, discussed and went through various draft structures until finally implemented in 1935. The communities were allowed to elect their first six representatives. The Archbishops appointed their 'experts', including the only woman on the Council, the renowned spiritual director Evelyn Underhill. The Advisory Council had come into existence.

Yet at the beginning, it was still seen very much as an interim measure. The Council was expected eventually to produce a set of Regulations. Communities would then, it was envisaged, one by one accept these and 'enrol at Lambeth' as formally recognised communities. Their reward for this enrolment would be that their members would all join the electoral roll for the next Advisory Council elections, due after seven years in 1942.

But communities remained divided as to their response. Some were prepared to go along with this scheme, others were adamantly opposed until further freedom of action was granted by the bishops. Communities which were more 'Roman' in their outlook, and, for example, used Latin liturgies, were particularly wary of signing up to any Regulations. Communities less anxious about such matters nevertheless felt unable to enrol as they saw the need for communities to act together. They did not wish some to be recognised and others not.

The Second World War provided a legitimate reason for not holding elections in 1942; yet, they could not have been held anyway as no community had 'enrolled' and hence there were legally no registered voters. Had the bishops insisted on such enrolment, the six representatives of communities would have resigned and the Advisory Council would have disintegrated with nothing to replace it. Its chair, Kenneth Kirk, the Bishop of Oxford, therefore advised the Archbishops to leave matters as they stood. The members of the Advisory Council therefore continued to serve. In 1943, they produced a set of guidelines for communities and bishops, the very first *Directory* (now renamed the *Handbook*). The guidelines were simply that – there was no compulsion, no sanctions for non-compliance, just suggestions for good practice.

In 1944, the bishops decided the Advisory Council itself could decide on the electorate for future elections to the Council. The *Directory* had been well-received by the bishops and they were content to abide by its contents. In turn, Religious communities without any compulsion saw the value of the *Directory* and in general showed loyalty to its regulations. In the present day of litigation it can be used as guidelines of recognised good practice.

In succeeding years, the Council evolved through its own decisions, most noticeably the possibility of women and lay Religious serving as community representatives. The Advisory Council has worked well over nearly seven decades. It remains advisory, with technically no possibility of imposing any decision-making power over communities or bishops. Yet, ironically, that is almost certainly the very reason its authority has been respected. The diversity of Religious Life has been allowed expression and yet the *Directory* has provided a stable foundation for maintaining the order and discipline of the tradition. Both bishops and Religious in the Church of England and in the wider Anglican Communion have reason to be grateful.

CHAPTER 1

THE RELIGIOUS LIFE

Jesus said to them, 'Follow me.'
(Matthew 4:19)

101 It is the calling of all Christians to be Christ-like. Sharing with other Christians in the baptismal mystery of Christ's death and resurrection, Religious are likewise members of the universal Body of Christ, but with a calling to live in community under the evangelical counsels of poverty, chastity and obedience, as their particular way of responding to the Gospel.

102 Religious communities, in that they celebrate the eucharist and live a common life inspired by the original apostolic community of which it is said, 'all who believed were together and had all things in common', and, 'they devoted themselves to the apostles' teaching and fellowship, to the breaking of bread and the prayers' *(Acts 2:44, 42)*, are themselves communities of the Church, sharing in its spiritual resources of faith and sacramental grace. However, they express their communion with the rest of the Church, apart from the structures of dioceses and parishes, through their own particular Constitutions and Rules and in relationship with their Episcopal Visitors.

Religious communities relate to one another as a communion of communities, within the communion of the Church, each one living out its own particular charism and objects, while all hold to their common foundation in the Gospel counsels of poverty, chastity and obedience. By this means the Religious communities aim to serve the Church by witnessing to the spiritual riches that are proper to all Christians. Today this combination of prayer and withdrawal, of study, of community life, often with apostolic works, has formed the basis of the Religious Life.

103 Religious communities vary widely in their practice of this way of life, reflecting the spiritualities of several pioneers of the past, whose written Rules have formed their particular ethos: St Basil, St Augustine, St Benedict, St Francis. However, they share the following common purposes:

i.   to build up the community in the Word of God before and on behalf of the whole human family in order to witness to God within and beyond all things;

ii.   to be signs, for those who have eyes to see, of the total commitment to which Christ calls all who would follow him;

iii.   by the offering of a Christian commitment to love both their sisters and brothers within the community, and their neighbour, to show forth the true value of human relationships;

iv.   to engage in the prayer of Christ to the Father and to offer the common worship of heart and mind, and in so doing to provide encouragement and inspiration to others;

v.   to give to its members the freedom to devote themselves permanently to the loving service of God within a disciplined common life;

vi.   to stand alongside the powerless poor, the exploited and the marginalised, not only through ministry but also in prayer, entering into their sufferings to whatever degree is possible.

104   To fulfil this commitment, and in accordance with their objects, the Religious communities may fruitfully render, alongside other Christians, such acts of service as:

i.   a care for the underprivileged, the unevangelised, the sick in mind or body or in other kinds of human need;

ii.   a provision for teaching and learning, and growing in the spiritual life;

iii.   a place for others to come, whether Christian or not, for temporary withdrawal from the pressures and demands of contemporary living, within an atmosphere of prayer and recollection;

iv.   a sharing of ideals and manner of life on an ecumenical basis or as part of inter-faith dialogue as opportunity affords.

Some Orders fulfil their objects by maintaining an enclosure so that they might give themselves more effectively to prayer and the contemplative life. As such they stand before God in solidarity with all Christians, and intercede in Christ for the whole world.

105   i.   For such monastic communities given to living the contemplative life the main work is the offering of the Divine Office together with periods of solitary prayer and *lectio divina*. For Benedictine communities the evangelical counsels are interpreted primarily in terms of life-long stability in the community for persevering in conversion of life. This is emphasised in their tradition by making vows in the specific form of stability, conversion of life and obedience. Wherever in the *Handbook* reference is made to vows or the evangelical counsels these terms should be applied to those communities with the meaning or form given above.

ii.   The superior of the community is the local 'ordinary' of the monastery or convent and is responsible for the Divine Office and eucharistic liturgy and the life of the community that flows therefrom.

106   The distinctive character and objects of a Religious community are defined in governing instruments such as a Constitution, Statutes or Principles. These are described within chapter 7 (Life in Community). Such communities are approved by the Advisory Council as 'recognised communities'. For the sake of clarity, a register of recognised communities is held by the Administrative Secretary to the Advisory Council.

A community that lives out its Rule and Christian witness but does not require its members to make a specific vow of celibacy, or a dispersed community whose objects do not include that of living a common life, may be approved by the Advisory Council as an 'acknowledged community'. A register of acknowledged communities is held by the Administrative Secretary to the Advisory Council.[1]

107   These and other newly-styled Christian communities are to be encouraged within the life of the Church and good communication and fellowship may be expressed and exchanged within such diversity as can be helpfully shared.

108   An individual who lives the consecrated life, such as a hermit or anchorite, who is not a member of a Religious community but who is committed by vow and Rule of Life made to a bishop, is recognised and considered in its own section of this *Handbook* (see Appendix VI). All such individuals are encouraged to identify themselves with the Advisory Council. A register of those living a consecrated life is held by the Administrative Secretary to the Advisory Council.

109   The purpose of these registers of recognised communities, acknowledged communities and of individuals is to assist communication between the Advisory Council and the bishops of the Provinces of Canterbury and York, where matters of procedure, advice or encouragement are required.

---

[1] Examples of these 'acknowledged communities' are the OGS (Oratory of the Good Shepherd) and CMP (Company of Mission Priests).

CHAPTER 2

ADMISSION TO THE RELIGIOUS LIFE

*When you search for me, you will find me; if you seek me
with all your heart.*
(Jeremiah 29:13)

201 A Religious is one who, having fulfilled the requirements of a community, has bound himself or herself by professing vows or promises to God, and has been admitted to membership of that community, with the rights, privileges and responsibilities as set forth in its Rule and Constitution. Before admission and profession can take place, the candidate's vocation must first be tested in the postulancy and noviciate of the community, in accordance with the community's Constitution. Each community should ensure that the training offered to the candidate is adequate for introducing the candidate into its own particular charism and calling from God and its interpretation of the evangelical counsels, and how these form the pattern and character of its common life and ministry.

202 A person who approaches a community, with a view to testing a vocation to its life, is commonly called an aspirant.

In preliminary discussion with such a person, attention should be drawn to possible difficulty in finding secular employment again in the event of not proceeding to profession. Enquiries should also be made regarding the candidate's financial obligations, insurance liabilities and pension provisions. The candidate should be free from any personal obligations that could conflict with the requirements of the Religious Life, for example, legal responsibilities towards a former spouse or children.

Candidates should make several occasional visits to the community while they are considering asking for admission. In approaching a community for which the observances of enclosure and silence are an important part of the Rule, it is helpful to both the aspirant and the community that the aspirant should have an opportunity to live for a time alongside the community before a decision is made to begin the postulancy (see paragraph **206**).

203 (a) No aspirant can be received while still legally a minor. It is important that any aspirant should have had time to complete their education and to acquire the basic skills of life and for earning a living. In the conditions which now exist, it would be unusual for an aspirant to be received earlier than their mid-twenties. Superiors and those responsible for assessing the suitability of candidates should ask for the names of persons willing to provide references on behalf of those seeking admission. It is desirable that one of these should be a priest.

(b) A certificate of baptism, and normally a certificate of confirmation, should be required. Reference should be made to other communities where the candidate may previously have tested a vocation.

(c) A certificate of health should be procured from the candidate's doctor, and the community is advised to require a medical examination by a doctor of its own appointment. It may be desirable that a psychological assessment is made.

(d) Ordained persons should not be received without reference to the diocesan bishop under whom they have most recently served.

(e) It may be wise to ask a postulant before admission to sign an undertaking not to sue the community for loss of wages or other benefits in the event of not proceeding to profession.

(f) Each community whose work involves the association of its members with children or vulnerable adults is now advised to obtain an 'enhanced disclosure' from the Criminal Records Bureau (CRB). This will be required for each new member who is invited to test their vocation, and others who intend to work under the direction of the community. This may be obtained either by registering the community with the CRB or through the diocesan office of the Mother house (see also Appendix IV).

Divorced candidates

204 Care should be exercised in the admission of a prospective postulant who has a divorced partner still living. When one partner has by divorce intended to free the other to contract another marriage, this action has also implicitly freed that partner to contract the vows of Religious profession. Nevertheless, there should be a sufficient distance between the divorce and the time the candidate is admitted.

Divorced persons may therefore be considered for admission to Religious vows. Such consideration may properly include asking to see the petition of divorce, and in all cases the community should satisfy themselves that the inquirer has not applied pressure on an unwilling spouse. If the candidate is a parent with children who are minors or in any other way dependent either financially or psychologically, they are not free to undertake the commitment to a Religious community.

Those considering admission of a divorced person to Religious vows should also bear in mind that a divorced person may mistakenly turn to the apparent security of a Religious community in order to compensate for the psychological wounds and loss of security produced by the divorce; and that a divorced person may be tempted to think of the Religious Life as an escape from perceived personal failure or from public discrimination against the divorced.

Responsibility for admission of a divorced person belongs to the community concerned, but the Visitor should be consulted at an early stage.

Trans-gender candidates

205 Advice is available from the Pastoral Secretary of the Advisory Council care of Church House, London.

Postulants

206 Unless the Constitution of the community states otherwise, the responsibility for inviting or refusing candidates belongs to the superior. An aspirant who is resident in the community and has been accepted is known as a postulant and, having been placed in the care of the novice guardian, will embark formally upon the preliminary course of formation and discipline which is required by the Constitution before admission to the noviciate.

Novices

207 A novice is a probationary member of a community who, being of required age and in satisfactory health, having shown sufficient maturity to undertake the life of the community, and having given adequate signs of a definite purpose and intention, has been admitted to formation and to training in its life and discipline.

Admission is accorded by the superior under such conditions as the Constitution of the community may require. In some communities admission to the noviciate is signified by the giving of the habit.

The rite of admission of a novice is a community, rather than a public, event, since it marks an entrance into training, not an acceptance into the Religious Life. It appropriately takes a simple form including the reading and exposition of scripture, perhaps within a community Office or other gathering, but not necessarily in church or at the eucharist.

208 The duration of the noviciate, preferably not less than two years and possibly longer, should be laid down in the Constitution, and provision made for the extension of this time where desirable, though with a clear limit.

There should also be provision regarding the circumstances and length of time for which a novice may be granted time away from the community without being obliged to begin the noviciate again.

See also paragraph **803** concerning the personal property of a novice.

209 Although as a probationary member the novice has no right to a determining voice in the government and administration of the community, the Constitution may provide for a share in its deliberations. The limits of such participation should be clearly defined.

210 The training of novices is the corporate responsibility of the whole community, but is normally and immediately exercised through the novice guardian and those designated to assist the novice guardian, working in consultation with the superior. All members of the community have an obligation to help novices share in the common life and to encourage them by the example of their lives and by their prayers. They must, however, take care not to interfere in the novice guardian's discharge of this personal responsibility (see also paragraph **903**).

211 Responsibility for recommending a novice for election to profession is normally shared by the superior and the novice guardian, who may seek the advice of members of the community who have been appointed to share in the novice's training and in the assessment of progress. In some communities such consultations are required by the Constitution.

212 The period of a noviciate may be terminated at any time by the community, in accordance with the provisions of the Constitution. A novice has the right to withdraw at any time from the noviciate, and may not be detained by the community against the novice's own will or judgement. Although on such dismissal or withdrawal all obligations created by admission to the noviciate cease, both for the community and for the novice, the community will properly have a continuing concern for the future welfare of the individual. It is pastorally desirable that prayer should be made with the novice at the time of departure.

CHAPTER 3

THE VOWS

*Offer to God a sacrifice of thanksgiving and make good
your vows to the Most High.
(Psalm 50:14)*

301 Religious profession is the liturgical, ecclesial and public act by which Christians can freely bind themselves to God through the vows of poverty, chastity and obedience, after due training, probation and acceptance by the community.

302 The substance of the vows is the gospel precepts as applied to the specific conditions of a Religious community consisting of women or men (or both), who have chosen lifelong celibacy for the sake of the Kingdom of God. In scriptural usage a vow is more than a legal undertaking. As promises made to God, these vows presume a mature dependence upon God, and on-going prayer for the grace needed to fulfil the self-dedication which the vows express.

The vows a Religious makes at profession are a public declaration to live out their baptismal consecration in this particular form of gospel living in the context of a Religious community.

Since these vows are made with the formal agreement of the community and often in the case of life vows also of the Episcopal Visitor, in the presence of the church in heaven and on earth, those who make them do not have the power to dispense themselves from the performance of them. Any dispensation or commutation of these vows must be granted by the competent spiritual authority as defined by the Constitution of the community.

303 Vows of religion are a condition of entry into a new mode of life. They carry the obligations of a life lived in dedication to God in accordance with the evangelical counsels of chastity, poverty and obedience, within the common life of a community, under a superior and a Rule approved by episcopal authority. The Benedictine tradition expresses this principle by using vows of stability, conversion of character, and obedience.

304 Poverty, chastity and obedience and in the Benedictine tradition, stability, in the context of a community have primarily a spiritual and ascetical purpose. They provide a way of training for celibate men and women who have heard the call of the Lord to deny themselves, take up their cross and follow Christ in this way. For those called by God, this will be the way they will grow into the personal fullness God intends for them. Yet they also have certain juridical aspects which relate the specific obligations of the vows to the context in which they are observed according to the Rule and Constitution of each community.

(a)   By the vow of poverty the Religious aims to follow Christ who 'though he was rich, yet for our sake he became poor' *(2 Corinthians 8:9)*. Seeking this dependence on God alone, and detachment from all material ties, Religious aim to share in the particular mode of simplicity of life set forth in the Rule of their community. This renunciation involves the voluntary stripping of all possessiveness, preparing the Religious to share with thanksgiving in the community's receiving from God all things necessary for their common life.

In learning to depend upon God for the material needs of their life, and to use all things for those purposes which are in accordance with God's providence, the community and its members can be set free to share their common life and prayer in Christ with all who come to them, and with those whom they serve in an external ministry.

The juridical aspects of the vow of poverty are set out in Chapter 8 (Property – paragraphs **803–810**).

Go sell what you own, and give the money to the poor, and you will have treasure in heaven; then come, follow me.   *(Mark 10:21)*

(b)   By the vow of chastity Religious undertake to present themselves to God for the sanctification of their whole being, so as to become a new creation in Christ.

In His life among us, Jesus renounced intimate sexual expression and the companionship of a partner. This is a costly discipline, which is the choice too of the Religious *(Mark 3:21, 31–35)*. Sexuality, the power to love and creative energy for relationships and union, are of His making. The Religious is called to be a

10

witness, celebrating and channelling the potential for love in the new fruitfulness of the Kingdom. This can be achieved only when the deepest self is anchored in God as Jesus Himself bore witness: 'I and the Father are one'.

The celibate life is one pathway to salvation that gives hope of attaining maturity and holiness as people who are loving, disciplined and free.

Truly, I tell you, there is no one who has left home or spouse, sisters, brothers, parents or children, for the sake of the reign of God, who will not receive very much more in this age, and in the age to come eternal life. *(Luke 18:29, 30)*

(c)   By the vow of obedience the Religious desires to grow in union with Christ, who sought not his own will but the will of God who sent him. They seek detachment from self-will, making this renunciation in a God-given spirit of faith and love. This is done through seeking to discern God's will in the requirements of the Rule, in the lawful demands made by the superior and other officers of the community, and in the discussions of the Chapter. The exercise of consultation and shared decision-making further underlines this fundamental character of the vows of obedience. This needs to be seen as a work of grace within the context of a common life in which the whole community is growing in their realisation of the will of God for them, in accordance with the particular charism and calling of that community.

Rights and claims of conscience are in no way restricted by the obligations of obedience, and any difficulties should be clearly and respectfully stated to those giving the order. A plea of conscience, however, cannot justify claims due to ignorance or self-will. In any grave difficulty regarding the vow of obedience, counsel should be taken, and in the last resort appeal made to the Visitor.

I came from heaven, not to do my own will but the will of the One who sent me. *(John 6:38)*

(d)   By the vow of stability the Religious undertakes to remain constant in relationship with God in the context of the Religious family to which the individual has been called, demonstrating publicly an intention of permanence of commitment, and providing a prophetic witness to the value of continuing relationship in a changing world.

11

In making this undertaking the Religious is aligned with Christ in his eternal mission to bring light and salvation to a world and culture absorbed by concerns of a transient and temporary nature.

I am with you always, even to the end of time. *(Matthew 28:20)*

305 Profession of vows within a community is a dedication of the whole person to God and also involves a contract of mutual obligation between the Religious and the Religious community. By profession the community admits the Religious to membership according to the provisions of the Constitution, and the Religious offers his or her life to God within the community according to its Rule and Constitution.

306 The formulae of profession should be set out in the Constitution. They should remain unaltered, except by recognised procedure laid down in the Constitution, to ensure that all members of the community are bound by the same terms of obligation to God and to one another.

307 Most communities provide for their members to make their life commitment under vows in two stages, the first at the end of the noviciate and the second after a period of further probation under vows, 'temporary or annual', or 'promises'. In some communities first vows are replaced by a form of promise, making a commitment to the life and practice of the community for a specified period, which may be renewable in accordance with the Constitution. The Constitution should define how the community relates these stages, the time limit for the first stage and the procedures for effecting the transition from the first to the final stage.

308 Profession under temporary vows normally takes place at the eucharist, after the gospel and homily, and should be considered as essentially a response to the gospel. The appropriate habit or other insignia may be given at this rite.

In a tradition that has grown up from earlier monastic procedures, a short period under temporary vows or promises is followed by life vows. The Chapter rights of the former will be in the Constitution. The latter admits the Religious to the privileges of full membership in the community.

The obligations undertaken at first vows or promises are binding with full effect until the specified time has expired, unless the Religious is dispensed by the appropriate authority and procedure as set out in the community's Constitution. When the time limit is reached the Religious either renews the first vows for a further specified period or proceeds to life vows, in accordance with the Constitution: or reverts to the secular state. Some communities do not specify a time limit for first vows and therefore they are not renewable.

309 At the close of the period spent in first vows or under promise, the Religious, if accepted by the community and wishing to do so, professes life vows, according to the provisions of the Constitution. Life vows (also called second, perpetual, final or solemn vows) are professed with the intention of lifelong obligation.

Life vows should be made with the most solemn of admission ceremonies in the presence of the community and people after the gospel and homily in the eucharist. A solemn prayer of blessing and recitation of litanies are appropriate.

Some communities may require and desire the presence of the Visitor or other representative at this most solemn ceremony. The Visitor attends to show the Church's witness and acceptance of the vows, but their presence is not otherwise required for theological reasons.

310 Members make life vows with the full intention of remaining in the community for life. Each community states in its Constitution the arrangements that need to be made regarding personal assets such as money and property. It needs to be clearly recognised by both parties that any monies made over to the community can in theory under civil law be re-claimed should the member depart. Therefore such assets should be regarded as an 'interest-free loan'. It is important that a document to this effect should be signed, noting the sum involved, and careful records kept.

Where a person is the owner of real estate and the community requires that they dispose of such property prior to profession, the direction of the Constitution is to be followed. This may involve a direct sale or the transferring the deeds of ownership to family members, etc. If the Constitution gives no guidance the person needs to discuss the matter with the superior and dispose of it appropriately. If the person wishes to give the property to the community, and the community is prepared to receive it, it is vital that legal advice is sought over the method of conveyancing, giving due attention to the complexities of current charity law.

For those communities that are also registered charities, other important documents for tax purposes that need to be signed at this point are 'Gift

Aid Declaration' or whatever is from time to time applicable. A will needs to be made at this time, e.g. naming the community as the recipient of the 'interest-free loan'. It will also enable the charity, on the member's death, to receive the money without inheritance tax.

CHAPTER 4

TRANSFERENCE

In my Father's House are many mansions.
(John 14:2)

401 Transference of a Religious in life vows to another community should be seen as a response to a call from God to that Religious in person to follow Christ more nearly in the way of the evangelical counsels within a different context from that in which the vows were originally made. Both communities involved need to be clear that this is the prime motive for any particular application for transference. Transference should not be resorted to because of incompatibility or lack of stability (see also paragraph **506(e)**).

402 Transference is therefore not a second profession. The form of reception should acknowledge the vows already made, while enabling the transferring Religious to express lifelong commitment according to the Rule and Constitution of the receiving community.

403 The chapter on transference in any community's Constitution should accord with the provisions of the *Handbook*, so as to avoid misunderstandings between any two communities involved in this process. It should also name the authorities for granting the permissions required, which should normally be the same as those granting permission for life professions within the community. In any particular case of transference the superiors of the communities need to compare the provisions of their respective Constitutions, and resort to the *Handbook* where clarification is needed regarding the process to be followed.

404 A Religious seeking transference to another community should submit a medical certificate or other evidence of general health and in particular of mental stability. The community in which life vows have been professed should grant leave of absence to cover the period of probation and training in the receiving community, and give an undertaking, should the plan of transference be abandoned, to receive the Religious back without prejudice or loss of status. Financial arrangements for the maintenance of a Religious during this period of leave of absence should be determined by the superiors of the two communities concerned. The two superiors should continue to communicate about the progress of the transferring Religious until the process has been completed.

405 A period of specific training is necessary to ensure that the transferring Religious has opportunity to absorb the ethos and way of life of the receiving community. The length of the period of probation and the conditions of training should be agreed by the authorities of the two communities concerned. This period should be not less than one and not more than three years. During the time of probation their status within and obligation to the original community are in abeyance and their new status within the receiving community is operative.

406 If, at the end of the period of probation, the transference is accepted by the receiving community, the consent of its Visitor is to be obtained. The consent of the Visitor and Chapter of the community in which profession was first made must also be obtained.

407 An appropriate proportion of any capital which the Religious gave to the first community at the time of profession may be transferred to the receiving community. The Visitors of the two communities shall jointly approve the appropriateness of such settlements. No other money need be transferred (see also paragraphs **803–805**).

408 Even at these early stages of testing of this new vocation, there should be careful pastoral co-operation when a Religious wishes to move from one community to another. Therefore when a novice or Religious in temporary vows transfers to another community there are no constitutional impediments since a fresh probationary period will be appropriate.

409 When a Religious applies to transfer to a community in another province of the Anglican Communion, due respect must be paid to any provisions concerning transference of Religious which may have been made by the ecclesiastical authority of that province.

CHAPTER 5

SEPARATION FROM THE COMMUNITY

I will trust and not be afraid.
(Isaiah 12:2)

Temporary separation

501 Temporary separation of a Religious from the community may take either of two forms: leave of absence or exclaustration. The Constitution of the community may also provide for categories of detached service that differ in substance from what is described here and would be an arrangement whereby a member is required to live away from the community for purposes of fulfilling a ministry or other objects of the community.

502 Leave of absence, other than prescribed regular holidays, is given for temporary residence outside the community, usually for a period of one year or less. The Religious remains subject to the authority of the superior and throughout the period of absence retains such Chapter rights as are allowed by the Constitution or otherwise directed by the Chapter.

(a) The Constitution should state who has the authority to give such leave of absence. It may be given in circumstances such as the following:

- the need to care for a sick or elderly relative;
- where a lengthy convalescence is required;
- in order to re-examine vocation;
- to explore experimental forms of Religious Life;
- for a specific work or study;
- for other causes resulting from physical, psychological or spiritual needs.

(b) In each case there should be a written agreement, negotiated with the community through the superior or Chapter who define the period of leave and the conditions upon which it is given. The following matters may be clarified in the statement:

17

- modifications to the rule of daily prayer (Divine Office, attendance at the eucharist and times of personal prayer);
- the wearing of the habit;
- relationship to the community during the period of leave;
- relationship to a local parish;
- financial arrangements;
- other matters relating to the observance of the Rule;
- the frequency of meetings to review the situation with the superior.

The signatures of the member and the superior express the agreement of each party to the modified Rule.

(c)   When leave is granted to an ordained Religious, or one who for other reasons holds a bishop's licence or permission to officiate in the diocese, the matter should be reported to the diocesan bishop. When a Religious takes up residence in another diocese during leave of absence, the diocesan bishop should be informed of their presence with some indication of the circumstances pertaining.

Generally, leave of absence is granted only to those in final vows. However, where a community is empowered to grant leave of absence to a member in simple vows, similar directions pertain, and it is recommended that a revised Rule of Life be agreed between the member and the superior, during the time of leave of absence.

Exclaustration

503   Exclaustration is permission for a Religious in life profession to live outside any convent or house of the community for a stated period, in the first place not exceeding three years. Normally after this time the Religious must either return to the community or ask for secularisation. The Visitor should be involved. Exclaustration is granted only for serious reasons and assumes a dispensation from the communal obligations arising from profession, unless otherwise stated in a Decree of exclaustration. It is a means of relieving the burden of obligations while retaining the support of spiritual fellowship and the guardianship of the vows. Extension of exclaustration beyond three years may be given by the Visitor at the joint request of the community and the Religious concerned. The length of each period of extension should be defined, bearing in mind that the longer the period away, the more difficult reintegration becomes.

(a)   The Constitution of the community should state who has authority to grant exclaustration. In each case there should be a written statement of the period and conditions, including financial arrangements. A decree of exclaustration should be drafted which sets out the conditions of separation (see (g) below).

(b)   Permission for exclaustration will first be considered by the same authority in the community as that which admits members to life vows. If consent is given, the Visitor must be asked to ratify the decision, who then authorises a decree of exclaustration for the period assigned. The decree is completed after the requesting Religious and also the superior have added their signatures.

(c)   Should the community not support an application for exclaustration, the Religious making the application has the right to appeal to the Visitor. The Visitor may wish to consult with the officers of the community and may, further, consult the Advisory Council before deciding how to proceed.

(d)   During the period of exclaustration the Religious remains bound to the vows and by such other obligations of the Religious state as are compatible with the conditions of life allowed during the period of exclaustration. Dispensation may, however, be granted from all or any of the particular forms of discipline prescribed by the Rule of the community, such as the recitation of the Divine Office. The habit will not normally be worn, and the community would therefore need to ensure that the member is provided with suitable clothing.

(e)   During the period of exclaustration the Religious takes no part in the government of the community and, if ordained, is subject to the Ordinary of the place of residence. The community should inform the diocesan bishop of any Religious who is granted exclaustration, and the necessary licence or permission to officiate regularised.

(f)   Exclaustration ends when the agreed period expires, or earlier if the Religious applies for and receives permission to return or applies for release and secularisation. If they return, all the general obligations pertaining to the membership are once again embraced.

(g)   A Decree of Exclaustration may be worded in the following or similar form:

In response to the application of (N) ...... and following the resolution of the community Chapter, (having obtained the ratification of .... (if the superior general has not otherwise been included in the decisions to date)), this Decree recognises the exclaustration of the above-named member, according to Paragraph 503 of *A Handbook of the Religious Life*, and with the following understandings of the superior and the member:

i.   concerning the length of the period of exclaustration;
ii.   concerning the financial status of the Religious (with any arrangements agreed);
iii. that the Religious will not bring the name of the community into disrepute;
iv. concerning the wearing of the habit or the distinctive cross of the community.

Having obtained the approval of the member and the superior, the Decree should be issued, signed and dated by the Visitor.

Permanent separation

504   Permanent separation may take either of two forms: release or dismissal. Both forms involve secularisation (see paragraphs **508–510**).

505   *Release* is an act of the community in response to a request from an individual Religious for separation from the community. Unless other provision is made in the Constitution, the decision to grant the release rests with the body by which election to profession was originally made. The decision given by that body should be ratified by the Visitor. It is advised that the Constitution states the detailed procedures to be followed to effect release. Release is effected by an Instrument of Secularisation (see paragraph **510**).

506   *Dismissal* is an act by which the community excludes from membership a professed Religious who persistently refuses to accept the obligations of the community as embodied in the Rule and Constitution. The community should assemble the evidence with care and record the circumstances. Grounds for dismissal would apply where a Religious:

i.   has publicly renounced faith;
ii.   has contracted a marriage without first seeking release;
iii. has abandoned the common life of the community and refuses to return after repeated admonition and persuasion.

In cases i. and ii., the community may need to proceed to an immediate declaration of dismissal. However, in case iii, care should be taken to note other factors that may be pertinent to the situation and if appropriate, the possibilities of transference or exclaustration explored.

(a) *Ecumenical factors*

If a Religious joins an ecclesiastical obedience not in communion with the See of Canterbury, release will normally have been requested. If release has not been sought, the community may need to proceed to secularisation.

In some cases change of ecclesiastical obedience may happen in conjunction with what is in effect a transference from one community to another (see chapter 4); but in others a Religious joining another obedience will wish to be secularised (see paragraphs **508–510**). The status of the consecrated life already being lived may become a matter of private vows of chastity, and possibly poverty, under the laws of the receiving Church.

(b) *Warnings*

In all cases of dismissal, the initiative lies with the community, and the procedure is that provided by the Constitution, which should include the right of the Religious concerned to appeal to the Visitor. The Religious must be warned in writing at least one month before the case is considered formally and must be given clearly-expressed reasons for the proposed dismissal. To become effective the dismissal requires ratification by the Visitor, who should ensure that every effort is made to promote reconciliation, and every aspect of the case fairly considered before making their decision.

(c) *Conditions of Dismissal*

The effect of dismissal in civil law may be detrimental to the community should the dismissed Religious be able to bring legal proceedings in respect of their dismissal.

(d) *Confirming Dismissal*

The process of secularisation follows automatically upon dismissal, because it expresses the community's authoritative declaration that the Religious concerned has no continuing obedience to the community or the Rule. The community should therefore obtain a decree of secularisation from the appropriate authority before confirming the dismissal.

(e) *Last resort*

Since a dismissed Religious may retain a subjective sense of vocation, dismissal should not be considered until all the possibilities of transference and exclaustration have been fully explored.

(f) *Notice to local bishop*

The Visitor or the superior of the dismissing community should communicate the facts of the case to the bishop in whose diocese the dismissed Religious takes up residence, together with the Visitor's own statement as issued to the community. Such pastoral care as may be necessary will be determined, after consultation with the Visitor, by the diocesan bishop concerned. If the dismissed Religious is ordained, the bishop may have to administer appropriate ecclesiastical discipline, according to circumstances.

(g) *Re-admission*

The community, in its continuing pastoral concern, should commend the dismissed Religious to the diocesan bishop and should maintain as close contact as is possible. If the Religious seeks re-admission to the community, the case should receive the most charitable consideration and the Visitor should be informed.

Responsibility towards ex-members

Go and may the Lord be with you. *(1 Samuel 17:37)*

507 There are various circumstances that need to be taken into account where there is permanent separation either through release or dismissal.

Any monies that the member may have made over to the community at the time of profession or has subsequently inherited legally need to be returned to the departing member, as any will they have made is not operative until death. If a person wishes to make a gift, on leaving, to the community from their returned assets they are free to do so.

Though the community has continuing spiritual and moral responsibility towards an ex-Religious, the statutes should nevertheless explicitly state that no claim for maintenance can be made on the community, so that the community may be protected so far as possible against legal or financial responsibilities. Redundancy and pension rights in secular law are invariably the prerogative of the employed person. However, as there is no employer/employee relationship in a Religious community, there is no obligation of this nature. It is advisable that communities should pay National Insurance for all its members so as to provide them with basic government provision.

Consideration should be given to the moral claim for the immediate, and sometimes the permanent, need of the person concerned. Care should be taken over such matters as pension and royalties, which the Religious may have accrued. Some Constitutions make provision for continuing financial support. The return of the habit, community cross and profession ring is required, but the community should be prepared to provide adequate secular clothing or sufficient money to purchase it, to a standard determined by the community.

Most Religious leaving the community will not have independent financial resources and so should make application for relevant government help (i.e. social security benefit, income support and housing allowance). The person may need short term financial help from the community.

There are legal restrictions governing the disbursement of charitable funds which are noted in Appendix V.

508 *Secularisation* is dispensation from Religious vows, which entails the return of the individual to the secular state. It may be an act of compassion to the individual, or a step made necessary by circumstances and effected by authority. Proceedings may be initiated by the community, the individual or the bishop under whose jurisdiction the Religious lives or proposes to live. The Visitor must consult both the community and the Religious concerned in the process leading to an Instrument of Secularisation.

(a) The Archbishop of Canterbury has supreme authority in the provinces of Canterbury and York for dispensing persons who are under life vows, though in some communities the Visitor of the community exercises this prerogative. Constitutions should state clearly whether the Archbishop or the Visitor has authority to grant dispensation from life vows.

The Archbishop's authority rests on the Ecclesiastical Licences Act 1533 (25 Henry VIII 21.3), which deals with the so-called 'legatine powers'. Those communities which recognise the authority of the Archbishop to dispense should forward these requests to him through their Visitor.

(b)   The Religious vows are indivisible whether of poverty, chastity and obedience or of stability, conversion of character and obedience and form a single contract with God and with the community (see paragraph **303**). Secularisation, following release or dismissal, always entails dispensation from all the vows.

Some dispensed Religious may wish to continue living as if under vows. It is advisable that such an arrangement be made only after a sufficient period has elapsed, say after two years, to allow a new start to be made without the encumbrance of the effects caused by possible negative circumstances which brought about their release. The making of a personal vow is discussed in Appendix VII.

(c)   When it appears that a Religious is fundamentally unsuited to the life of the community, secularisation may be an act of justice, but undue precipitancy should be avoided, since experience of living in the world may lead a secularised Religious to understand that the real remedy lies in personal conversion and the return to the Religious Life in the former or another community.

(d)   Psychiatric disorder or severe psychological disturbance may necessitate the consideration of secularisation in certain cases; but the greatest caution is necessary. Diagnosis by, and medical advice from, a consultant are essential. If the treatment prescribed by the consultant is unsuccessful, it may be more appropriate to consider exclaustration. Although eventual secularisation may come as a great relief to some sufferers, for others the mere suggestion may be irreversibly damaging. It is almost bound to lead to a loss of self-esteem. Therefore, if secularisation is discerned to be the best way forward, careful efforts must be made towards rehabilitation in secular society. This is important not only for the excluded individual, but also for the psychological well-being of the rest of the community, where feelings of guilt and anxieties provoked by the separation may arise.

(e)   Secularisation should not be considered unless it is reasonably certain that the community is not able to make adequate provision for the sick Religious and that recovery of health cannot be expected. It is generally expected that communities will make provision for a frail or elderly member with any kind of health problems within the community. For their better care, they may be placed with professional carers. The advice of a consultant should be sought at every stage.

509 When a Religious chooses to separate from his or her community and moves to another province of the Anglican Communion outside the Church of England without having obtained dispensation from the obligations of Religious profession, the following principles should be applied:

(a)   The community, in consultation with its Visitor, should decide whether the Religious should be secularised, or should be invited to receive such direction as may make possible the maintenance of the obligations of Religious profession.

(b)   If the process of secularisation is initiated by the community, a statement of the case should be forwarded through the Visitor to the bishop of the diocese in which the Religious resides or proposes to reside. After receiving that bishop's comments, the community will finally decide whether to transmit the application to the Archbishop of Canterbury or to the Visitor, according to the provisions of its Constitution.

(c)   If the process is initiated by the bishop of the diocese in which the Religious is living, the community should refer the matter to the Visitor in order that the Visitor's opinion may be secured. The Religious concerned must also be given adequate opportunity to make representations. With the facts thus ascertained, the community will decide whether secularisation is appropriate, and will forward the case to the Archbishop of Canterbury or return it to the Visitor for decision, according to the provisions of its Constitution.

(d)   If the process is initiated by the Religious concerned, the community must ensure that the bishop of their place of residence is kept fully informed of the proceedings.

(e)   In all cases, notice of dismissal must be sent by the community to the Religious concerned and to the bishop of their place of residence.

510   Formula for an Instrument of Secularisation:

Whereas N ..., known in religion as N ... of the community of ... *within our metropolitical jurisdiction*, has made application for secularisation (or has been deemed by the community to require secularisation), we ... by divine providence Archbishop of Canterbury, (or we ... Visitor of the community, acting in accordance with the Constitution or Statutes of the community), after full examination of the matter do hereby dispense and release him/her from his/her vows of religion and declare him/her to be no longer a Religious.
    Given under our hand, etc.

* * These four words are omitted if the instrument is signed by the Visitor.

CHAPTER 6

CHAPTER GOVERNMENT

Test everything; hold fast to what is good.
(1 Thessalonians 5:21)

601 The Chapter is the seat of government of a community and an integral
and vital part of its corporate life.

Here it learns to be a part of the Holy Spirit's leading into a fuller
realisation of the truth of its vocation.

When the Spirit of truth comes, he will guide you into all the truth.
(John 16:12a)

Each community's Constitution will formulate guidelines, which are to be
adhered to by that particular community.

In principle, a Chapter is not merely a legislative and decision-making
body but also a forum where issues pertaining to the community's life
and the pastoral care of its members may be discussed. In all discussions,
the members of Chapter will want to show a generous concern for one
another in furthering their common vocation.

602 Membership of the Chapter is defined by the Constitution of each
community. This will state who may attend and who has voting rights at
particular Chapters.

603 The Chapter represents the whole body of the community, being bound
by its Rule and Constitution, and has responsibility for holding together
the tradition and the ongoing developing life of the community, 'like the
master of a household who brings out of his treasure what is new and
what is old' *(Matthew 13:52)*.

The corporate mind of the community is expressed when it meets in
Chapter, presided over by the superior or another as designated by the
Constitution. Whether or not the Chapter includes all professed members,
it is representative of the whole body. It is bound by the Rule and

Constitution and has responsibility both for the tradition and also for the developing life of the community.

604 It is important that there should be freedom of debate in Chapter meetings. Informal discussions, questionnaires and referenda may be useful in preparing for debate in Chapter, but the results should not be used as the equivalent of votes. Decisions on all important matters should be taken by vote after open discussion in a meeting of the Chapter.

605 Some of the functions of the Chapter may be delegated to councils or committees. If this is done, the different functions of such councils and committees should be clearly defined in the Constitution.

606 The Constitution should clearly state all matters relating to the Chapter, including:

(a) the qualifications for membership of the Chapter;

(b) the functions to be discharged by the chairperson in the government of the community; and the responsibility of the superior to the Chapter and the relation of the whole community to Chapter decisions;

(c) distinctions between different kinds of Chapter, such as greater, ordinary, general and special;

(d) the manner in which the Chapter is to be convened, including such matters as due notice, written agendas and reports;

(e) the frequency of meetings (there should be at least one annual meeting of the ordinary Chapter);

(f) special rules governing the Chapter summoned for the election of a superior;

(g) the relationship between the various Chapters, community councils and committees that may exist and the composition and function of such councils and committees.

607 The duties of these Chapters may include:

(a) the election of the Visitor;

(b) the election of the superior;

(c) elections to profession;

(d) decisions on questions of separation from the community;

(e) alterations to the Rule, Constitution or Statutes;

(f) decisions relating to the disposal of property or expenditure of money as required by Chapter;

(g)   decisions on the beginning or closing of important activities or work of the community, including the foundation and closing of houses;

(h)   decisions on beginning new ministries.

608   Meetings of the Chapter should begin and end with prayer, being aware at all times of its responsibility under God for the ongoing life of the community.

(a)   Due notice as required by the Constitution should be given beforehand to each member who has the right to attend, together with a copy of the agenda.

This notice and agenda should be sent whether the member is expected to be able to attend or not. Where the interests of an individual member are concerned (such as in a question of separation from the community) due notice must be given of the method by which the matter will be brought to Chapter, so that all concerned may have adequate time for prayer and reflection.

(b)   A meeting of the Chapter should be presided over by the superior or other person defined by the Constitution. The chairperson is responsible for maintaining the statutory and customary rules of procedure; for securing full exercise of rights of discussion for all members, whatever their rank or age, with impartiality and justice; and for expediting the business of Chapter. The right of all members to speak without fear or favour must be secured; and they should exercise this right with humility and respect.

The chairperson may present a personal view of any matter under discussion, but is not entitled to impose this view on the Chapter.

(c)   The Constitution should state clearly which members are entitled to vote in elections to office, elections to profession and other Chapter business.

(d)   The Constitution should also state which members are eligible for various offices in the community.

(e)   The Constitution should state all who are qualified to vote and the methods of voting. The Constitution must also define what constitutes a majority in elections:

Either the elected candidate shall be the one receiving more votes than any other or such other majority as the Constitution requires.

(f)   The Constitution should make provision for securing the votes of those who by reason of permitted absence or other legitimate cause are not present at the meeting where votes are taken. This provision applies particularly to electoral voting, where the procedure is normally by secret ballot and without discussion, and also to voting for changes in the Rule and Constitution.

The Constitution should define whether the vote of an absentee may be recorded either in writing or by the appointment of a proxy.

(g)   All members are bound in conscience to seek the will of God for the common good and to exercise their vote in this sense without regard to private interest or personal prejudice.

(h)   The rules of procedure at Chapter meetings should ensure that matters of importance cannot be introduced without notice under the heading 'Any Other Business' unless the matter is recommended by the chairperson for an emergency debate.

The Constitution should provide that emergency debates may only be held if they are approved by the chairperson and a majority of members of the Chapter at the beginning of the meeting.

(i)   The superior may be required by the Constitution to seek the authority of the Chapter for certain courses of action. In these matters the superior is bound by the decision reached in Chapter, unless exception is provided in the Constitution.

(j)   The agenda, attendance and minutes of each meeting should be recorded and the adequacy of the minutes duly attested by agreement of those present, the minutes being signed by the chairperson.

609   The Visitor may need access to Chapter records and to all other records in matters of dispute that are referred to them.

CHAPTER 7

LIFE IN COMMUNITY

Let the foundations be strongly laid.
(Ezra 6:3 AV)

701 Governing Instruments

(a) *The Rule* of a community is a document setting forth the spiritual, disciplinary and moral principles based upon the Gospel by which the lives of all the members are to be ordered. Explicit acceptance of the Rule is an integral part of the act of profession.

The Rule may have another name, and may consist of the Principles of the community's life, organisation and spirituality, often composed at or near the time of the community's foundation, and possibly owing much to classic rules.

When the Rule is mentioned in profession or other formal ceremonies, no room for doubt should be left as to precisely which document or documents are intended.

Whatever its title, the Rule is in most communities an historic document and a focus of community identity and loyalty. The Constitution should make clear how, if at all, the Rule can be changed.

(b) *The Constitution* is a body of enactments, of a legal nature, usually called *Statutes*, by which the life of a community is administered. The Constitution should have a preamble setting out the aims and objects of the community, and should include all the matters in the schedule appended below (paragraph **702**).

Some communities use the word Statutes for the sections of the Constitution. Others use it to refer to a separate series of detailed enactments that can be revised more easily than the Constitution, but will not be inconsistent with it.

In other communities the document called the Constitution governs the whole national or international body of the community, while the word Statutes is reserved for documents that apply at local or provincial levels within the community.

Since the usage of these terms may vary, references to Constitutions in this *Handbook* should be taken where applicable, as referring also to Statutes in communities where the Constitution and Statutes are separate instruments.

Although the idea of a Constitution and Statutes drawn up in formal and legal language may seem repugnant to a community living according to the gospel of grace, there is sound reason for requiring every community to have an adequate Constitution. A good Constitution promotes the purposes of the community and protects the interests and the freedom both of the community and of its individual members. It is a means whereby corporate unity is maintained, and provides a basis for relating to other legal entities.

Moreover since the Church of England does not provide a section in its Canon Law for the governance of Religious communities in general, it requires rather that the Constitution of every particular community should include all that is necessary for this purpose. This *Handbook* aims therefore to pass on a sound tradition of good governance as already proved in the experience of existing Religious communities.

While these general directives need to be applied to the particular circumstances of each community, their application should nevertheless maintain as far as possible a common terminology comprehensible to the Church at large. This common terminology is appropriate to communities which are, or hope to become, registered Religious communities of the Church of England.

The *Handbook* provides for the wide variety of the Religious communities of the church. In particular community Constitutions however, there will need to be different emphases, say, in respect to the ordering of Chapter government or the Divine Office, as between a monastic community living in one place under the leadership of an abbot or abbess and a community of brothers or sisters living a more dispersed life. Each community will have its own structures for ordering its common life and worship, and for expressing its service to the Church and the world at large. The

Handbook aims to make a common provision which includes these differences.

Every member of the community should be familiar with the Constitution before professing vows, and copies of it should be made available to professed members. Failure to observe these points may jeopardise the community in cases of dispute, such as appeals against dismissal.

The Rule and Constitution form the ground for the covenant relationship entered into by the community with each of its members at profession.

(c)   The *Customary*, sometimes called a Handbook or house rule, is a body of regulations by which the daily domestic life of a community house is ordered. It has neither the spiritual weight of the Rule, nor the legal force of the Constitution, and its provisions can be altered with minimal formality by the superior or the Chapter, acting within the powers given by the Constitution.

702 Matters to be considered for provision in the Constitution (Not all these headings apply to every community):

1.   *The aims and objects of the community*
2.   *Community obligations*
       (a)   holy eucharist
       (b)   choir Office
       (c)   silence and prayer
       (d)   work
       (e)   enclosure
               (i)   character
               (ii)   regulation
               (iii)   permission to leave
       (f)   recreation

3.   *Visitor* (see also chapter 10)
       (a)   appointment
       (b)   term of office
       (c)   retirement
       (d)   unrestricted access of community members
       (e)   extent of responsibility
       (f)   provision for

        (i)   visitation (see also chapter 11)
        (ii)   appeal
        (iii)   other duties

4.   *Superior*
    (a)   by whom and how elected
    (b)   duration of office
    (c)   provision for termination of office
    (d)   duties and rights
    (e)   relation to Chapter (and council if there is one)
    (f)   duties in appointment of administrative officials

5.   *Administrative officials*
    (a)   duties
    (b)   qualifications
    (c)   how and by whom appointed

6.   *Chapter* (see also chapter 6)
    (a)   constitution
    (b)   functions and authority
    (c)   matters on which superior is bound by its vote
    (d)   president
    (e)   qualifications for membership
    (f)   duration of membership
    (g)   by whom appointed or elected
    (h)   manner of convening
    (i)   fixed times at which Chapters are to be held
    (j)   special rules of procedure
    (k)   character of votes required for specific objects
    (l)   method of voting
    (m) votes of absent members
    (n)   method of reckoning majority of votes

7.   *Council* (if there is one) (see also chapter 6, paragraph **605**)
    (a)–(m) as in 6 above
    (n)   relation of council to Chapter

8.   *Foundation and closure of houses*

9.   *Warden or chaplain-general* (where applicable)
    (a)   by whom and how appointed
    (b)   duration of office
    (c)   re-appointment

    (d)   termination of office
    (e)   responsibilities and duties in regard to
        (i)   superior
        (ii)   Chapter
        (iii)   chapel, services, etc.
        (iv)   chaplains
        (v)   community works, branch houses, etc.
        (vi)   matters on which the warden has a right to vote
        (vii) rights of access and appeal

10.   *Chaplains*
    (a)   by whom and how appointed
    (b)   duration of office
    (c)   re-appointment
    (d)   termination of office
    (e)   responsibilities and duties in regard to:
        (i)   warden
        (ii)   community
        (iii)   other persons

11.   *Confessor extraordinary*
    (a)   by whom and how appointed
    (b)   duration of office
    (c)   re-appointment
    (d)   termination of office
    (e)   responsibilities and duties in regard to:
        (i)   warden
        (ii)   community

12.   *Aspirants and Postulants* (see also chapter 2, paragraphs **202–206**)
    (a)   who accepts
    (b)   minimum age for admission
    (c)   requirements (e.g. health, ecclesiastical recommendations, baptism, confirmation)
    (d)   duration (minimum and maximum)
    (e)   dismissal and by whom

13.   *Noviciate* (see also chapter 2, paragraphs **207–212**)
    (a) (b) (d) (e) as in 12
    (c)   freedom to leave

14.   *Profession* (see also chapter 3)
    (a)   by whom elected and on whose initiative (at each stage if there be

more than one)
- (b) minimum age (at each stage)
- (c) quality of vows
  - (i) temporary
  - (ii) temporary leading to perpetual
  - (iii) perpetual
- (d) formula of profession
- (e) what authority may grant dispensation
- (f) rights and privileges of professed (in the case of temporary leading to perpetual)
- (g) minimum and maximum period of duration
- (h) conditions of renewal
- (i) terms of release or dispensation
- (j) authority granting permission for perpetual vows

15. *Transference* (see also chapter 4)
- (a) by whom permitted
- (b) method of both sending and receiving
- (c) with what effects

16. *Separation* (see also chapter 5)
- (a) leave of absence
  - (i) by whom
  - (ii) with what effects
- (b) exclaustration
  - (i) by whom
  - (ii) with what effects
- (c) secularisation
  - (i) procedure
  - (ii) by whom granted
- (d) dismissal
  - (i) procedure
  - (ii) conditions
  - (iii) financial provisions

17. *Property* (see also chapter 8)
- (a) community property
  - (i) its nature
  - (ii) by whom legally owned
- (b) individual property
  - (i) administration of property of novices and those in temporary vows
  - (ii) whether members retain possession or not

        (iii)   members to make their wills on profession or not
        (iv)   property acquired after profession
        (v)   management of life interests
        (vi)   royalties and copyright

18.   *Oblates, tertiaries or associates*
    (a)   conditions of acceptance
    (b)   regulations
    (c)   obligations
    (d)   dismissal
    (e)   resignation

19.   *Dissolution of the community* (see also paragraphs **802, 907, 1003** and chapter 13)
    (a)   when required
    (b)   care of residual members
    (c)   disposition of property

20.   *Alteration or suspension of the Constitution, including experimental change*

703   The Divine Office

Religious communities have traditionally used orderly recitation of the Psalter as the core of their daily prayer. Bible readings, readings from spiritual writings, songs (both hymns and responsories) and prayers are added to the psalms in regular daily liturgical worship. This daily corporate prayer is known as the Divine Office and forms part of the life of every community.

The precise form and content of the Office is determined for some communities by the Rule or the Constitution. In other communities this decision rests with the Chapter.

The obligation of attendance at the Office prayed in common, or of private recitation, should also be defined by the Constitution or Rule.

704   Enclosure

The enclosure or cloister is that part of a community's house and grounds which is reserved for the sole use of the members of the community, to ensure necessary privacy and quiet. The extent of the enclosure and the regulations which govern it vary with the character of the community.

The enclosure should be clearly marked off from the rest of the house and property. Rooms for the reception of guests and day visitors, or for transacting business, should be clearly designated.

Most communities assign a room or cell to each member for sole occupation. Its purpose is to provide complete privacy. The Rule or the Customary should determine regulations about the use of the cell, and will reflect the community's attitude towards the ideals of solitude and silence.

Where the degree of enclosure is a mark of the community's Rule, it may still be necessary for non-community members to enter and work within the enclosure. The Constitution should also regulate permission for community members to leave the enclosure.

705 Recreation

Every community, paying due regard to the provisions of its Rule of life, should ensure that adequate daily and weekly periods of relaxation, both corporate and individual, are provided. Regular attendance at communal recreation strengthens the life of the community; free time for the individual is a psychological necessity.

Members of the community should also have adequate annual holidays, suitable to the character of the life.

706 Association with the Community

A community may make provision for those who wish to be associated with its prayer and work, while following a calling outside the community. Their association with the community may be expressed in different forms, among which are those traditionally known as oblates, associates and companions. Oblates were originally distinctive of the Benedictine tradition, closely bound to a particular monastery. They have been instituted and adapted by other communities. They do not profess vows but make promises for such periods as the Constitution of the community determines.

Some oblates or associates may live in the Religious house with which they are associated, sharing, in such measure as may be appointed by the appropriate authority in the community, the life and worship of the community. Such persons are usually described as intern oblates or interns.

Alternatively they may live apart from the community in a society of their own, with a Rule and Constitution provided by the community.

Oblation and association may also be a means whereby oblates or associates follow the ideals of the community while remaining in their own state of life. They accept a degree of authority from the community in their spiritual lives, observing a personal Rule of life administered by the community, to which they are closely bound in prayer.

707 Some communities may wish to integrate into their lives groups of persons not living under Religious vows. This plan may involve a modified form of internship, with or without promises, and on an informal basis. Sensitivity is required to protect the integrity of the Religious Life. Where housing is involved a tenancy agreement is recommended.

708 A third order (whose members are usually called tertiaries) is part of the Franciscan tradition, and involves a Rule of life and commitment by the members to each other. This constitutes a separate order, parallel to and closely connected with the community, but distinct from it.

709 Any person who is closely identified with the community and who engages in the community's ministries will be subject to similar scrutiny as for community members themselves, and it is the responsibility of those in authority in community to obtain the required level of check (see Appendix IV).

CHAPTER 8

PROPERTY

No one claimed that any of the possessions were their own;
they shared everything they had.
(Acts 4:32)

Property of the Community

801 Every community is required to make sufficient and adequate
arrangements in law for the property and other fixed assets for which it
has stewardship and responsibility. This will be through a Deed of Trust,
or public or private trustees, or by a Scheme of the Charity
Commissioners, or by the inauguration of a company limited by
guarantee. The Constitution of the community, which
in some established communities does itself act as a foundation
document, should define how these may be held. Where appropriate,
communities should register with the Charity Commissioners and due
attention should be given to the current recommendations in regard to the
requirements for the preparation and auditing or independent examination
of charity accounts and the responsibilities of charity trustees (on which
helpful guidance is available from the Charity Commission). Competent
legal and other professional advice should be sought in all decisions
regarding the purchase and sale of all fixed assets, including the
services of an estate agent in respect to realty, and an investment manager
in regard to public investments. Negotiating adequate cover by insurance
against loss or damage to the community's assets is a further
responsibility of trustees or Chapter.

Role of Trustee

802 Trusteeship of a charitable Fund carries specific responsibilities, whether
that Fund is of the Order to which the sister or brother belongs or some
other Fund to which the member has accepted the role of trustee. It is
therefore important that individual trustees understand these
responsibilities and assess whether they are competent to undertake the
role.

All trustees are required to be familiar with the community's governing documents and understand that the role carries legal duties and financial responsibilities. They may only act to assist the charity to achieve its aims and objects.

Where appropriate therefore, new trustees should be selected according to a clear policy of recruitment which should also give guidance concerning selection and the training of trustees in their duties. At all times 'best practice' and processes which are transparent should be seen to be operating in all area of public accountability.

Pertaining to Religious communities in particular, professional skills as well as wisdom and discernment are required at a time when a community can no longer sustain its life or fulfil its stated objects. Communities are advised to have included in the governing documents the procedures in the event of closure. (see also chapter 13: Closure). Considerable assets may be involved and, in so far as assets need to be disposed of, charity law will generally require them to be disposed of for the best price reasonably obtainable, without any right on the part of other communities to lay claim to them. Thought therefore needs to be given to the possibility of including provisions in the Constitution under which, if the community closes, its net assets can be given to some other community or communities, in order to avoid their having to be sold on the open market, as a means by which the objects of the community may in some form continue. The Advisory Council may be invited to assist in the earlier stages of consultations, though the trustees will work closely with the community members, the Visitor and local advisers. In all cases, professional advice is essential to the carrying through of such matters.

Property of individual Religious

803 (i) Novices and Religious in temporary vows retain the legal ownership of their personal property, which, however, they administer only with the permission of the novice guardian, superior or Chapter. They may be required to pay for their maintenance, but may not alienate any property without express permission, nor make over any of it to the community.

(ii) On profession in perpetual vows, a Religious will dispose of personal assets, in the spirit of the evangelical vow of poverty and to the extent that this is required by the community's Constitution. When this is done, the needs of the natural family and others to whom the Religious is tied, as well as the needs of the community, are considered. The Religious will assure the community that the task of 'renouncing all possessions' has been duly completed.

804 The assets any individual member makes over to the community at the time of life profession together with any subsequent legacies or inheritances made to them personally legally may be claimed, should the member leave. Therefore it is advised that such monies should be regarded as an 'interest-free loan' to the community. There need to be signed documents to this effect clearly stating the amounts involved. There should also be separate records kept. The money may be invested or used by the community but funds must be reasonably available to replace the capital if required in the event of that member withdrawing from the community.

The Central Board of Finance of the Church of England Funds are collective investment schemes established by the Church Funds Investment Measure 1958 (amended in 1995). They are available to Anglican Religious communities registered in England for deposit and investment purposes. However, monies that are deemed in law to belong to an individual cannot be so deposited or invested with them, unless they are held by the community on the 'interest-free loan' basis described in the paragraph above. There are several choices of other Funds available for investing or depositing community monies available to communities though they must represent a secure investment with acceptable interest yield.

No constraints may be put on a Religious to endow the community beyond the extent of a contribution to the common funds of a community made at profession, when such is required by the Constitution. Beyond this, the Religious remains a free agent in the disposal of personal property. Equally, there is no constraint upon the community to accept any endowment or benefaction. However, it would seem prudent that any member, having considerable assets to dispose of at life profession, should consider making an interest-free loan to the community, of at least such an amount as would be needed to re-establish themselves in the unexpected eventuality of their being released from the community.

805 In the case of income, whether regular or capital, which is received or earned by a Religious, the community's Constitution should state how such items are received and receipted. Salaries, stipends, royalties and pensions are normally received and accounted for by the community. Sometimes the amount of income tax deducted from personal income may be recovered by the Religious community, and advice may be sought from the charity division of the Inland Revenue or other adviser. A legacy bequeathed to a Religious would, unless otherwise stated in the Constitution, be directed to the funds of the community, or, if the legatee so authorised, be assigned to a third party. Where a Religious is the beneficiary of a life interest, the basis on which the income is accepted should be agreed between the member and the superior. The appropriate community officer should then be informed of the arrangement, so that due regard to be given to all the parties involved, including the reversionary owners.

806 Some communities permit their members to retain ownership of property in their own names, even after making a life commitment. In such cases it is advised that the administration of their assets be so arranged as to cause the least disturbance, both materially and spiritually, to the member and community alike. The community's Constitution or Statutes should direct the means of appropriating such sources of income between the common fund and elsewhere. An attested will should be completed by the member, which settles their property at the time of death.

807 Royalties and other income that will continue to arise after the death of a member should be the subject of a clear agreement in law (such as the member's will) that identifies the recipient of these funds.

808 Where a Religious receives gifts for a specific project in relation to a work or ministry to which they become attached and which is outside the community's financial accounting, it is desirable that proper records are maintained and submitted to the appropriate authority. Regular reports should be offered to the superior or Chapter in order that they may be kept informed of the situation.

809 A Religious will not retain a gift for personal use without seeking guidance from their superior or Chapter.

810 The means of attracting funds to provide for and maintain the community when members reach old age should be carefully considered and reviewed. It is strongly recommended that communities pay National Insurance contributions to enable each member to be entitled to whatever government benefits that may be available (i.e. state pension). Voluntary contributions to the state or other pension schemes may provide regular income for the community in future years. Other state benefits are available to a Religious who may be assessed as incapacitated and/or requiring regular attendance, and such income should be applied and accounted for by the community. Professional advice should always be sought when in doubt.

Copyright

811   Copyright is normally vested in the individual creator of an original work, e.g. a musical composition, artwork, articles, etc. Within a Religious community two factors should be noted in particular.

Firstly, a member professed under vows will normally wish any personal copyright to be assigned to their community. In this case there needs first to be a document setting out the relationship between the two parties (the register of profession will suffice). Further, to make the assignment legally effective it is advised that a simple Deed of Assignment be signed and witnessed. In it the member declares that he or she has assigned to the named community the copyright in all works which may have been made, written or composed since the date of their profession.

Secondly, permission to reproduce a work for which the community holds a copyright may, at the discretion of the superior or Chapter, be given with an acknowledgement in writing accompanying the work reproduced. A statement on the following lines should suffice: 'Copyright in [   ] is owned by the Order/Society/Community of ... by whose kind permission it is reproduced.'

812   Where a copyright permission is sought, the community should make the appropriate application for permission from the copyright owner or licence authority. For education and research purposes it is acceptable for a small portion of a work to be copied by the person giving or receiving the instruction – but not by reprographic process. Reproduction of material for general use, e.g. the copying of a song for a time of worship, would require either the permission from the copyright owner or the cover of a licence. Many groups find it helpful to purchase an annual licence, e.g. the Church Copyright Licence (CCL), allowing the licensee to reproduce hymns and worship songs or combine the CCL with a Music Reproduction Licence (MLR), to photocopy music from authorised publications. (Details of the Church Copyright Licensing (Europe) Ltd (CCLI) may be found under 'Useful Addresses'; also the address for Calamus, a Roman Catholic copyright agency.)

Tenancy

813   Communities intending to offer accommodation for a set period of time should be aware of the rights and legalities which pertain to such matters and should seek appropriate legal advice. Tenancies fall into two categories: residential and commercial. In the case of residential letting any written agreement should be drawn up on the basis of an 'assured short hold tenancy' which enables the owning party to recover possession of property without hindrance of any lawful rights of the tenant. All offers of accommodation should be subject to the signing of the appropriate document, and occupancy should not commence until this has taken place. A commercial tenancy (that is, for business use in the widest sense) does require careful negotiation, and legal advice should be sought in drafting a formal tenancy agreement. It is when tempted into an informal tenancy arrangement that the community can discover, and be held to, unforeseen rights which favour the tenant. This should be strongly resisted. Also the Charity Commission expect the community to gain proper financial benefits from their assets, and where a tenant is offered a discounted rent, it must be in fulfilment of the objects of the community and where such an act of charity can be justified.

Tied Accommodation is the term applied when a property is occupied in return for a range of duties. The letting of a property to an employee may attract a Benefits-in-kind charge for Income Tax purposes. To overcome this factor the need for the employee to be resident has to be demonstrated. Any rights of spouse or family need to be clearly stated in the tenancy agreement or the contract of the one employed.

Property on Licence/Lease of Property: Letting property 'on licence' is a form of occupancy which falls some way between an assured short hold tenancy and a lease. The drafting for this sort of agreement is complex and requires legal advice.

CHAPTER 9

OFFICERS AND EMPLOYEES

*Guard that which was entrusted to you with the help of the Holy Spirit
who lives in you.*
(2 Timothy 1:14)

901 The principal officers of a community are the superiors and novice
guardians. Others may be required by the Constitution.

902 A superior is one to whom responsibility for the common good and the
good of each member is entrusted by constitutional appointment, usually
by election. Different areas in this constitutional responsibility are
expressed by specific titles such as superior general, assistant superior,
provincial superior, and superiors of branch houses. Every superior
exercises a ministry of oversight and service towards the members of the
community. In certain traditions special terms are used for superiors, such
as abbot, abbess and prior/ess among the Benedictines; minister and
guardian among the Franciscans; leader, director and other terms in other
communities.

903 The novice guardian is a Religious to whom is committed the formation
of novices in the Religious Life (see also paragraphs **210** and **211**).

The novice guardian is the superior's deputy in regard to novices and
must therefore act within the bounds laid down by the Statutes and in
obedience to the superior. The superior should ensure that the novice
guardian has reasonable freedom in the exercise of this delegated
authority.

The novice guardian should not be assigned any duties which might
impede the primary obligation of caring for the novices. If novice
formation is assigned to a team, the novice guardian should co-ordinate
the work of the team in consultation with the superior.

The superior and Chapter should be kept regularly informed about the
progress of novices.

The manner of appointment of the novice guardian should be defined by the Constitution.

904   If the Constitution requires a warden or chaplain-general, it should also specify the method of appointment by the community. It should be clearly understood that such appointments are made to serve the appointing community and not the appointee. Should a matter of concern or dispute arise, either the community or the warden should consult the Visitor and the Advisory Council.

The functions of a warden or chaplain-general should be clearly defined in the Constitution, with explicit provisions relating to:

(i)   appointment;
(ii)   rights and duties;
(iii)   term of office;
(iv)   the possibility of reappointment;
(v)   retirement;
(vi)   the possibility of removal from office;
(vii)   relation to other priests, such as assistants, chaplains and confessors.

An ordained person appointed to such a post and residing within the diocese requires an appropriate licence or permission to officiate from the diocesan bishop, unless the bishop's licence is already held in respect of some other ecclesiastical post. An ordained warden residing outside the diocese must hold a licence or permission to officiate from a diocesan bishop.

It is inadvisable for a community's Constitution to multiply the number of external officers by specifying assistant wardens, sub-wardens or other functionaries.

905   A warden or chaplain-general should not expect the community they serve in this capacity to conform to their personally-held views on various issues.

906   It is not advisable to have the warden or chaplain-general as a trustee.

907   In this position of trust, particular care needs to be taken in cases where the community is moving towards planning for closure. Responsible arrangements must be made for dealing with the community's property and financial assets according to charity law; the wishes of the remaining members and the original aims and objectives of the community.

Ample provision must be made for the full ongoing care of the members and their wishes regarding how they live out the rest of their Religious lives must be honoured, for example, they may wish to transfer to another community. Any receiving community should be assured of receiving adequate provision for their ongoing care, particularly for their latter years and possible incapacities, from any remaining assets.

The warden or chaplain-general must not benefit personally, nor any enterprise or project they are personally engaged in, from the disposal of the community's assets.

908 Where a community wants to appoint a chaplain, the chaplain needs to be licensed by the bishop of the diocese. The rights and duties of the chaplain in relation to the warden and the community should be clearly defined in the Constitution, or by some other means, e.g. in a resolution of the Chapter. There should be a written contract stating the length and conditions of the chaplain's appointment. If accommodation is provided in the community's property refer to paragraph **813** Tenancy when drawing up the contract. To ensure that the contract is consistent with the requirements of employment law the contract should be drawn up with the advice of their solicitor.

909 Communities, particularly those which are enclosed, may appoint a number of confessors, some Religious and some secular priests, giving the members of a community freedom of choice and the right to resort to any of those appointed. It may be advisable that priest members do not hear the confessions of members of their own community.

Superiors should not normally hear the confession of members of their own communities.

The confessors should be experienced in hearing confession and knowledgeable about the obligations and requirements of the Religious Life. In no case has the confessor, as such, any right to intervene in the internal or external affairs of the community or to dispense from any part of the Rule.

910 Individual Religious may be permitted to choose as spiritual director some suitable person other than the priests who minister to the community. A formal approach to a spiritual director who is not an officer of the community should be made only after receiving the superior's approval.

911 Important posts such as Bursar, Infirmarian and Archivist should be held by competent people within the community or be employed or appointed by it. In the case of employees there needs to be a contract which clearly states the terms and conditions of employment. It should also state to whom they are responsible and the method and frequency of reporting. A job description and a clear written understanding of each particular job enable good responsible stewardship regardless of the status of the one holding the post.

912 Professional advice and assistance are more necessary than ever before in this time of complex new legislation and possible litigation. Skilled and experienced professional people should be engaged to assist in such matters as finance, investments, insurance, the administration and maintenance of property, legal and medical affairs.

913 For all salaried officials and regular employees of the community, especially those provided with accommodation, a contract of employment should be carefully drawn up with the advice of a solicitor.

914 New legislation regarding the duties and responsibilities of employers is continually coming into effect. It is the employer's responsibility to ensure that they know and implement all current legal requirements and good practice. It is important that all conditions regarding such matters as 'Health and Safety', and adequate insurance liability are covered and implemented.

CHAPTER 10

COMMUNITIES AND ECCLESIASTICAL AUTHORITY

They entrusted themselves to the one who judges justly.
(1 Peter 2:23)

1001 Every community must have an episcopal Visitor. Visitors are the guardians of the Constitutions of the community and guarantors to the Church at large of the community's sound administration, stability and right to confidence. In order to safeguard both Visitors and communities it is recommended that bishops should not accept this role for more than five communifies at any one time.

1002 The Visitor must be a bishop extraneous to the life and membership of the community. Another title may be used e.g. in Franciscan usage the title Protector is used.

(a) The Visitor's authority extends to all houses of the community, except those situated outside the jurisdiction of that national church. Other community Provinces or Houses in other countries normally would have their own Visitors duly appointed in accordance with the Constitution of the community. Visitors are the normal court of appeal for the maintenance of the community's discipline.

(b) Visitors should be chosen by the community. Some communities' Constitutions require them to have the bishop of the diocese in which the foundation headquarters or Mother house is situated. In cases where the Visitor is not the diocesan, their consent is needed for the appointment of another bishop from within the province; and that of the metropolitan should they be a bishop outside that province.

The Constitution of the community should contain provisions regulating the manner of appointment of the Visitor and specify matters or occasions on which their intervention is required.

(c) Before accepting the appointment, Visitors should familiarise themselves with the ethos and work of the community; with the details of the Constitution relating to their responsibilities and the precise extent of their authority; and the current condition of the community. If they have not already acted as Visitor to another community, they should inform themselves as to both the theological and legal status of Religious communities in the Church of England, so that when called upon to make judgements they may do so on the basis of sound principles.

(d) The Advisory Council on the Relations of Bishops and Religious Communities is available to assist Visitors, especially those newly appointed. Every community is asked to inform the Secretary of the Council promptly when a new Visitor is appointed, or reappointed, together with the term of office. The Secretary will then send the Visitor a copy of the *Handbook* and the annual reports of the Advisory Council. The term of office and the conditions for retirement should be laid down in the community's statutes.

(e) Visitors have the inherent right to make visitations at their own discretion. They should make visitation at least once in every five years in order that they may satisfy themselves on all matters of which they are guardians and guarantors.

(f) Visitors also have the right and duty of hearing appeals, whether addressed to them by the Chapter, or privately submitted by any professed member of the community, or by any responsible person external to the community, recognised by the Visitor as being a proper person to appeal to them. In the event of a formal written complaint being received by the superior, the latter will submit a copy to the Visitor and keep them informed of all the subsequent action. If the superior is unable to resolve the matter, the Visitor is the next level of appeal (see paragraph **1407iv**). Constitutions should make it clear that every professed member of the community has the right of unhindered appeal to the Visitor.

(g) Beyond the functions described above, whether inherent or statutory, the office of Visitor does not convey any right of intervention or initiative in the affairs of the community. Therefore the Constitution of any community should make clear the precise function of the Visitor.

(h) Under no circumstances should the Visitor expect a community to conform to personally held views on different topics.

(i) If a community declines to accept the advice of its Visitor, especially with regard to the provisions in the *Handbook* about the Constitution, both parties should report the facts to the ACRBRC. The Advisory Council will consider the matter and may advise the House of Bishops and if necessary, initiate a review of the situation.

(j) Should a community's Constitution require the consent of the Visitor to be changed and the Visitor refuse against the wishes of the community, the community may appeal to the ACRBRC, who would act as mediator.

1003 Particular care needs to be taken in cases where a community is close to or in the process of closure (see also chapter 13: Closure). Arrangements regarding the assets of the community, either in property or financial, are to be settled in accordance with the community's original aims and objects and with the wishes of the remaining members. All such arrangements need to be consistent with charity law.

The Visitor, therefore, will ensure that arrangements are made for the proper transfer of the temporal treasures of the community and the future care of the community's archives.

Visitors must not benefit personally, nor their diocese or any enterprise or project they are personally engaged in, unless such beneficiaries are within the remit of the community's charity, its aims and objectives.

It is of the uttermost importance that the Visitor sees that where possible the Chapter has made adequate provision for the full care of the remaining members. Their wishes regarding how they spend the rest of Religious lives should be provided for. Any receiving community should be assured of receiving proper provision for their care from the remaining assets.

1004 Religious are subject to the ordinary jurisdiction of the bishop of the diocese in which they reside. 'Ordinary' is a legal term derived from Roman civil law, describing jurisdiction that is inherent in the rank or office (Latin *ordo*) held and is not delegated. So far as Religious communities are concerned, this means that ordained Religious are subject to the provisions of statute and canon law, in particular with regard to licences and ecclesiastical discipline.

Every community should possess a copy of the Revised Canons Ecclesiastical kept up-to-date. Superiors and ordained Religious should take particular care to be familiar with the canons. The superior of the community is the 'local Ordinary' of each of its houses and is responsible for the Divine Office, the eucharistic liturgy and the life that flows therefrom.

1005 Religious who exercise a ministry within a diocese must hold the appropriate licence or 'permission to officiate'. They are responsible to the diocesan bishop for their public actions and utterances.

1006 The superior should consult the bishop before moving any Religious who holds a diocesan appointment.

1007 In the Church of England, ordained members of Religious communities have no exemption from episcopal oversight and only limited privileges, such as participating in the election of the communities' clerical representatives to the General Synod; but the bishop's oversight does not involve any right of intervention in the internal affairs of a community.

1008 Many non-ordained members of communities carry out various ministries that come under the general heading of 'Pastoral Care'. These ministries may cover areas such as spiritual direction, spiritual accompaniment, counselling, and pastoral visiting. It is desirable that members should be appropriately trained for this and be under some type of supervision. It is helpful if a community has its own guidelines for pastoral care and practice. As it will be the perception that Religious are related to the diocese in which they minister, it is important to know and to comply with any diocesan guidelines in place.

Any Religious who is working with children, young people or vulnerable adults should have CRB enhanced disclosure clearance and should be familiar with national and diocesan child protection policies and comply with their requirements.

1009 A community which proposes to take up residence in a diocese, whether it be re-locating a Mother or main house or opening a branch house, should consult the diocesan bishop at an early stage in its planning. The diocesan bishop will consult with the local parish priest and clergy. Likewise the community should inform the diocesan bishop of its intention to move or close a house within their jurisdiction.

1010 A Religious who is assigned as an assistant in a parish is responsible to the parish priest in all matters relating to parochial work. There must be a written agreement between the community and the parish priest, including a formal job description with provision for payment, dismissal and withdrawal. This agreement must also make clear the extent of the community's responsibility for ordering the life of the Religious concerned and should define relations between the parish priest and the community.

A similar agreement should be made with the diocesan bishop when a Religious is appointed as an incumbent of a parish.

1011 Similar agreements should be formalised with cathedral Chapters, colleges, schools and other institutions to which Religious may be sent to minister.

1012 The diocesan bishop may license a minister to perform the Offices and services of the Church of England in any college, school, hospital, or public or charitable institution, including institutions maintained by Religious communities (Canons B41.2 and 3; and C8.4). If no such licence is issued, the institution remains within the cure of the local incumbent.

1013 Religious in holy orders who are assigned by their community to parochial or diocesan work are subject to the same episcopal jurisdiction and canonical obligations as the rest of the diocesan clergy.

1014 A diocesan bishop may admit to holy orders, without any parochial or other title, members of Religious communities living in houses within the diocese (Canon C5.2e). Candidates for ordination from Religious communities will be interviewed by the bishops' selectors under the auspices of the Archbishops' Council's Ministry Division, subject to any special circumstances, which are a matter for the discretion of the ordaining bishop and the Visitor of the community concerned. The most likely exception will be a candidate who would expect to exercise the ministry wholly within the community's houses. Applications for this special procedure should be made by the community Chapter to the Visitor. On the Visitor's recommendation, the ordaining bishop may then consult the Ministry Division. Bishops should bear in mind that a lay Religious may be tempted to seek ordination as a precaution against possible separation from the community or closure of the community. It is to be hoped and desired that the call a Religious may feel towards ordination is in fact a further deepening of the primary call and commitment to Religious Life.

1015 Some communities with houses in different dioceses have requested and used the ordination selection procedure through the diocese of their Visitor. This can be of great benefit to the community as it offers a more unified approach.

CHAPTER 11

GUIDELINES FOR EPISCOPAL VISITATIONS

By Wisdom a house is built and through understanding it is established.
(Proverbs 24:3)

1101 The New Testament account of the visit of Mary to Elizabeth provides a model for understanding the nature and opportunity of a Visitation. This is three-fold: firstly, the grace of mutual encouragement; secondly, a relationship which recognises the gift of life and the quickening power of the Spirit, often in that which lies hidden; and thirdly, thanksgiving for the 'wonderful works which God has done'.

1102 Historically the reasons and purpose behind Visitations have been and are to offer spiritual and pastoral support, encouragement and challenge. When preliminary discussion is taking place in preparation for a Visitation, it will be helpful to consider the current priorities and problems. There are also occasions of particular need or crisis when the Visitors will need to work closely with a community through a difficulty but that will not be a normal Visitation.

1103 The effectiveness of a formal Visitation is dependent on the relationship which exists between the Visitor and the community. It is therefore desirable that there be opportunities at other times for more informal visits and mutual exchange.

1104 The primary role of the Visitor is that of episcopal guarantor to the Church at large of the community's right to the Church's confidence and the community's guide in maintaining that confidence (see also paragraph **1001**).

1105 While a community will wish to keep its Visitor informed of major events and changes in its life as they happen, nevertheless, a formal Visitation provides the Visitor with the opportunity to be assured of the community's faithfulness to its Rule and Constitution, so that they may guarantee this to the Church and reassure the community of this trust.

1106 A Visitation may take many forms. What works for one community at a particular stage in its history may be inappropriate and unhelpful at another time. It is therefore essential that due recognition is given to the particular ethos and evolving nature of a community in order that the Visitation may serve to quicken the gift of the Spirit and make known the hidden works of God. Communities are therefore encouraged to draw up their own guidelines. The mutual co-operation between the Visitor and the superior in preparing for the Visitation is of utmost importance.

1107 The more the whole community is involved in the process of planning and preparation the more effective will be the outcome of the Visitation for all concerned. Consultation between the Visitor and the community over such matters as timing, the appointment of assistants, the structure of the Visitation and the areas of the community's life to be covered by it, is highly desirable and to be encouraged wherever possible. The community needs also to recognise its responsibility in helping the Visitor to prepare as fully and effectively as possible.

1108 In advance of the Visitation the following information should be available to the Visitor and the assistants if they do not already have it:

(i)   a copy of the Rule and Constitution;
(ii)   a list of all the members of the community, with age and date of profession;
(iii)   audited or examined accounts of the community for the last financial year, if the community is a registered charity and accountable to the Charity Commission – otherwise for the last three years (see Appendix II).

1109 Depending on the form the Visitation is to take, it may be helpful to gather information in advance in the form of a questionnaire. It is advisable that such a questionnaire be drawn up in consultation with the superior and his/her Council (see Appendix I).

1110 The Visitor will need to spend several days with the community and be prepared to visit all the community houses. If this is not possible for practical reasons, it is desirable that the assistants visit. The more time spent with the community by the Visitor and the assistants, the better the community will be served.

1111 The Visitor may be formally welcomed in the chapel or Chapter room. The degree of formality should be agreed between the Visitor and the superior. The Visitor may at this juncture address the community explaining their expectation of the Visitation.

1112 The method followed for the Visitation will have been decided by the Visitor and the community. Although every member of the community may not be seen, any who wish to see the Visitor must be allowed to do so. The assistants may see all the officers of the community as directed by the Visitor, and any others who specifically ask to see them.

1113 One of the community or conventual eucharists may be presided over by the Visitor during the Visitation.

1114 At the end of the Visitation, the Visitor may meet with the community to give a summary of the team's considerations. However, both in preparing this and the final charge, the Visitor will be advised to check comments and suggestions with the superior and perhaps some members of the council or Chapter. In this way making recommendations that would be impractical or contrary to the ethos of the community may be avoided.

1115 It is preferable for the Visitor to send the full report/charge in written form after the conclusion of the Visitation. Alternatively, it could be delivered to the community at a later date. In either form, the final document should be received within three months of the end of the Visitation.

1116 A Visitation may lead to the Visitation team making recommendations for the consideration of the community and its Chapter. These are recommendations only. However, matters which highlight any deviation or disregard of the Rule and Constitution by the community, or a member of it, are to be noted and acted upon.

1117 The superior should ensure that all members of the community have a copy of the Visitor's report/charge.

1118 When the community has had adequate time to consider the Visitation charge, a written response should be made to the Visitor. This would include any changes which have been made or decided upon as a result of a recommendation. Where the community has decided not to accept a recommendation, it may be helpful to the Visitor to be informed of the reasons for this.

CHAPTER 12

NEW COMMUNITIES

Behold I make all things new.
(Revelation 21:5)

1201 Along with the renewal of existing communities, the Holy Spirit may be expected to call into being new forms of Religious Life for responding to the needs of the times. While welcoming such new experiments, the Church may usefully offer them support and guidance, and put them to the test of perseverance in the hope that they can bear the fruit of the Spirit in the on-going development of the Religious Life in the Church before enrolling them along with the established Religious communities.

It should be recognised that the difficulties of a common life under vows are not immediately apparent to those without experience of it, and therefore it is important that such new communities grow by stages and are willing to draw upon the experience of the past as embodied in existing communities and upon the guidance of the Advisory Council.

1202 The granting of recognition by the House of Bishops will be a gradual process beginning when the community first approaches a diocesan bishop. The Advisory Council should thereafter be kept informed of the community's growth and development. Vows binding for life should not be taken before the Advisory Council has agreed to this.

1203 The following guidelines are proposed for the development of a new community as steps to be taken on the way to official recognition:

(a)   Members of a new community should first live together under a simple Rule in order to test their capacity for a corporate life and to clarify their aims.

(b)   When the corporate life has reached a stage at which its aims and distinctive spirituality can be formulated, the advice of the Advisory Council should be sought in drafting a Rule and Constitution.

(c)   When the community has lived under the Rule and Constitution for at least a year, the Advisory Council should be asked to approve the establishment of a noviciate.

(d)   The duration of the noviciate need not be determined precisely at this stage; but after a period of not less than two years, the community, after consultation with the Advisory Council, should advise the diocesan bishop of their wish to elect a Visitor to authorise admission to annual vows or promises.

(e)   These annual vows or promises should be renewed for at least three years, and if necessary for a further period until there are at least four members who have completed three years in annual vows. Life vows may then be taken with the agreement of the Visitor.

(f)   When there are seven members in life vows application may be made through the Visitor for recommendation by the Advisory Council that the community be officially recognised by the House of Bishops.

(g)   During the initial stages leading up to life vows, the members of the community should make over all personal income for the maintenance of the community while retaining their personal property in their own names. Community property should be held by trustees, and the trust deed should indicate how this property would be disposed of were the community to come to an end. In the transition period towards official recognition, the Constitution of the trustees should be settled with the advice of the Advisory Council. Advice should be sought also about the advisability of applying for registration as a charity (see paragraph **801**).

1204   When a group within an already existing community proposes to found a new community, the bishop of the diocese in which the new community proposes to settle should consult the Visitor of the parent community and the Advisory Council. The Council should seek to assess the maturity of this group and the motivation for their move so as to advise whether any time should elapse before the proposed new community is permitted to receive novices or admit to profession, and what stages of development might be needed to proceed towards recognition as a new community.

CHAPTER 13

CLOSURE OF A COMMUNITY – CALL TO WITNESS TO THE PASCHAL MYSTERY

O give thanks to the God of heaven: for his steadfast love endures for ever.
(Psalms 136:26)

1301 The vocation of a community is always to seek to be obedient to the will of God. As well as being faithful to the charism of its founding members and to the Spirit of its Rule, each community is called to be alert to the 'signs of the times' and to be continually searching to follow God's will in the age in which we are living. The time may come when the community has completed its particular vocation. However difficult or painful the process of bringing to a close a community's life and ministry, it must always be remembered that both for the community and its members the goal is resurrection not survival.

1302 The reality of the present time seems to be that many communities will have fulfilled the purpose for which they were founded. Falling numbers and the lack of aspirants may reduce a community to such a small size that there is no hope of recovery and the fact of imminent dissolution has to be accepted and worked with. This may come about earlier through the inability to fulfil its vocation, cope with the physical work required or to care properly for elderly or infirm members. But when a community has been reduced to four in number and there have been no new members in the last three years this suggests that definite action needs to be taken in discerning and planning for amalgamation or dissolution.

1303 The Constitution should state who will make the final decision about closure. This would normally be the Chapter. There could be circumstances which require the Visitor to take the initiative but this must be done in full consultation with any remaining members and with the advice of the ACRBRC.

The Visitor carries a responsibility for ensuring that the arrangements regarding assets of the community, either property or financial, are dealt with in accordance with charity law, the community's original aims and objects, and with the wishes of the remaining members. The Visitor, therefore, will ensure that arrangements are made for the proper transfer of the temporal treasures of the community and the future care of the community's archives. Visitors, their diocese or any enterprise or projects in which they are personally engaged are not to benefit directly from any of the assets of the community, unless such work or projects are in line with the fulfilment of the aims and objects of the community.

This is also the case for any warden, chaplain-general or chaplain (see also paragraph **1003**).

1304 A community with ageing members and a lack of new members needs to recognise and accept with courage the need to make decisions concerning the closure of the community, and to make adequate provision for remaining members.

Members will need time and support to accept the reality of the situation. They will have a whole range of responses – grief, pain, relief, anger, fear – and these need to be recognised both inside and outside the community. It is important that community members do not feel they are having advice and solutions imposed upon them as they plan for the future.

One of the factors that may need to be dealt with is other people's unreal expectations of the community.

1305 The Advisory Council needs to be informed and there is a need for the Visitor and warden/chaplain-general to be helpful and supportive at this difficult stage. The use of an external and experienced facilitator could be helpful together with suggestions from the ACRBRC.

1306 In order for this situation to be as life-giving as possible, this process needs to start early enough to allow for possible amalgamation or other suitable arrangements providing for the final and adequate care (financial and physical) of remaining members. Making adjustments of this magnitude stands a better chance of being life-giving if they happen when members are able to be as flexible as possible in order to adapt. As a general rule people find it more difficult to adapt to new living situations as they grow older.

1307 The Constitution of every community should contain provisions for dissolution in the event of the community becoming so small that it is unable to manage its own affairs. Legal advice needs to be obtained to ensure that any obligations, legal or moral are fulfilled. Where the community is a charity, or any of its funds or property are held in full or in part of a charity, it needs to be remembered that any dissolution or disposal of assets need to comply with charity law.

Provision needs to be made for the full and proper maintenance of members both before and after the community's closure. The increasing cost of the possible need for extended care in senior years, with the likelihood of increasing disability, needs if possible to be provided for. This is the case whether the future care of members is with some other community or within the provision of the local authority.

1308 The Constitution should also state what arrangements, bearing in mind charity law, if applicable, are to be made regarding the handing on or disposal of the community's property and assets. The disposal of property and assets in all cases needs professional guidance which will be required in the possible setting up of any trusts for the ongoing support of surviving members. This may be allowed by the terms of the original charity or may require the forming of a new charity (see also paragraphs **802, 907** and **1003**).

One of the community's important assets is their Archives. It is essential to honour the community heritage and to make sure that suitable arrangements are made for them. They should be duly set in order and placed with a recognised body for safe keeping. Advice may be sought from the county or diocesan records officer, from the Librarian and archivist at Lambeth Palace, London, or directly from the Royal Commission on Historic Manuscripts (see Useful Addresses).

1309 There are several ways in which a community might be enabled to plan for positive closure which could be a living example of new life and ways of functioning with diminishment. The earlier such possibilities are able to be explored and planned for, the greater the chance of their bearing fruit.

Some possible ways:

a)   One or more remaining members of a community to seek transference to another community as a way of fulfilling their vocation.

b)   To continue to live the vowed life as an individual outside a community. Vows may need to be transferred to the bishop of the diocese in which they are living. In this case the Visitor would inform the relevant diocesan.

c)   Another community may be able to accommodate the remaining members enabling them to continue to live together as a group as long as possible.

d) A community may be able to retain a suitable house to live in but this should not be done as a way of evading making a final decision about the existence of the community.

e) Particular pastoral sensitivity needs to be shown to the elderly and infirm especially if this involves them being placed in residential or nursing care when a community is no longer able to give them suitable care.

f) Some communities have obtained a dwelling in a retirement village to enable their members to stay together as long as possible but this usually requires other active members to give support.

1310 When the decision has been made to move towards some kind of closure it is important that there be a suitable event celebrating the life and witness of the community. This would honour and give thanks for the community and the faithfulness and commitment of all the members and associates living and departed.

Thanks be to God.

CHAPTER 14

GUIDELINES ON NEW LEGISLATION AND OTHER PROCEDURES

Everything should be done in a fitting and orderly way.
(1 Corinthians 14. 40)

1401 New to this edition is some basic information to highlight legislation that has recently been introduced and concerning which trustees, superiors and Chapter members need to be aware, and for which they are likely to be held responsible.

1402 Data Protection
The Data Protection Act 1998 came into force on 1 March 2000. Where personal data of identifiable living individuals is kept, it must be shown that the rules of good information handling (known as data protection principles) are maintained. Personal data covers both facts and opinions about a person, and also the purposes or intention for holding such information. At all times this must be processed fairly and lawfully.

Essentially the law is there to protect the subject against the careless use or actual misuse of their personal data. Therefore it gives rights to the subject to give consent to the use of such data and restricts the controller to legitimate and necessary usage, according to the purposes for which the information is held. The Act also makes special provision for the processing of sensitive data. Sensitive data includes religious belief, health, political opinion, ethnic origin, criminal proceedings and other personal matters. In general this may be held only with the explicit consent of the subject, and in compliance with legal requirements, and/or to protect the vital interests of the person concerned.

The Act allows individuals to apply for copies of personal data held about them. This is known as the right of subject access. When information held is no longer relevant to the controller (e.g. when a member withdraws from the community) it should be destroyed. If the community holds personal data on computer, it may need to submit a formal notification to the Information Commissioner. Each community has a legal obligation to comply with the Act. (See Useful Addresses for website and information line.)

1403 **Gift Aid** is a Government scheme which came into operation on 6 April 2000 (replacing the old Deeds of Covenant) whereby a charity may recover income tax from any pecuniary gift received from a tax-paying donor. The basic requirement is that the donor signs a simple declaration stating that *I wish* ... (charity's name) *to treat all donations I make to them from the date of this declaration as Gift Aid,* (or *the enclosed donation I make to them,* or *all donations I have made to them since 6 April 2000*). The donor should not generally benefit from the gift, though a small percentage is acceptable.

1404 **Health and Safety**
Where communities are dealing in any way with the public it is necessary to be aware of the requirements and restrictions to which a community may be subject and the liabilities that follow.

Particular aspects to be attended to relate to fire precautions, adequate control of health and safety risks arising from the work-place, and ensuring that you are maintaining safe plant and equipment. (Information line and address for Guidance packs: see Useful Addresses.)

1405 **Risk Assessment** is a requirement of S.O.R.P. (Statement of Recommended Practice, Accounting and Reporting by Charities as revised in 2000) to be undertaken by a charity that is obliged to undergo a professional audit, i.e. where the annual income exceeds a quarter of a million pounds (at the time of publication). Basically the community is asked to show that it has considered the many aspects of risk involved in running the charity and has a record of how it has taken steps to minimise those risks. The actual Risk Assessment is not published but is included in the checks made by the auditor. (See Charity Commission website under Useful Addresses.)

1406 **Employment of more than five persons**
The Welfare Reform and Pension Act 1999 includes a provision which requires any employer of more than five persons to have a stakeholder pension scheme in place. That would include a community employing more than five persons in a full-time or part-time capacity. It then becomes the employee's choice as to whether he/she decides to join the pension scheme. Where they opt to do so, the employer is responsible for deducting the contributions from their wages and passing this on to the pension provider.

1407 A Formal Complaint

A superior needs to be aware of the procedures that should be followed if a complaint is made by a member of the public against a member of the community. The following is offered as such a programme and every superior is encouraged to adopt something for their own use that covers the necessary ground, and also to incorporate this within a wider 'Code of Practice' to be followed by community members so as to minimise the risk of such things happening.

i.   Where the complaint has been made verbally, the superior should firstly inform the member concerning whom the complaint has been made with the detail of the complaint. At this stage all efforts should be made to resolve matters.

ii.   If they wish to proceed, a written document must be requested from the complainant, setting out the precise nature and circumstances of the complaint. If no written document is received the matter is concluded.

iii. On receipt of the written complaint the superior will inform the member, and provide a copy of the complaint for the member.

iv.   The Visitor should be informed as well as the chaplain-general or warden. The Visitor may be the best person to offer support and advice to the superior and to be available to hear any appeal.

v.   If the complaint is of a sexual nature, the community's code of practice or the diocesan guidelines should be strictly followed. If there is obvious risk of scandal the advice of the diocesan press officer should be sought.

vi.   Various meetings need to be arranged so that the superior may ascertain the facts and investigate the substance of the complaint. The superior may choose someone for his/her support. The member against whom the complaint is made may also name someone for his/her support. A brief record should be kept of these meetings.

vii. The superior will form a written summary from the meetings held with the hope of furthering a resolution and promoting reconciliation. Both the complainant and the member are informed of the appropriate action to be taken and each should indicate within a given time-span whether the outcome is acceptable. Each also has a right of appeal to any decision taken which would be directed towards the Visitor. It may be necessary at this point or earlier to obtain legal advice.

viii. The pastoral care of the member and wise counsel for the superior are essential at all stages of the investigation. It is equally important that the community shows both fairness and courtesy to the complainant, without prejudicing the situation, and that a line of honesty and integrity is maintained. If the matter is likely to lead to court proceedings, legal representation becomes necessary.

USEFUL ADDRESSES

Advisory Council on the Relations of Bishops and Religious Communities (ACRBRC)

The Administrative Secretary, Central Secretariat, Church House, Great Smith Street, London SW1P 3NZ.
Tel: 020 7898 1379

The Pastoral Secretary, c/o Central Secretariat, Church House, Great Smith Street, London SW1P 3NZ.

Anglican Religious Communities (ARC)

The Secretary, c/o Central Secretariat, Church House, Great Smith Street, London SW1P 3NZ.
E-mail: arc@fish.co.uk

Anglican Religious Communities Year Book

The Editor, c/o Anglican Religious Communities, Central Secretariat, Church House, Great Smith Street, London SW1P 3NZ
E-mail: pd10008@cus.cam.ac.uk   Website: www.orders.anglican.org/arcyb/

Archbishops' Council – Ministry Division

Ministry Division, Church House, Great Smith Street, London SW1P 3NZ.
Tel: 020 7898 1000
Website: www.cofe-ministry.org.uk

Care & Housing of Elderly Religious Project (CHERP)

Same address as **the Conference of Religious**:

The General Secretary, PO Box 37602, The Ridgeway, London NW7 4XG.
Tel: 020 8201 1861;   Email: confrelig@aol.com
Website: www.corew.org.uk

Charity Commissioners

Charity Commission contact centre telephone number: 0870 333 0123
Website: www.charity-commission.gov.uk/publications

Risk Assessment:
Website: www.charity-commission.gov.uk/supportingcharities/charrisk.asp

London: St Alban's House, 57–60 Haymarket, London SW1Y 4QX.
Liverpool: 2nd Floor, 20 King's Parade, Queens Dock, Liverpool, L3 4DQ.
Taunton: Woodfield House, Tangier, Taunton, Somerset TA1 4BL.

The Church of England

Website: www.cofe.anglican.org

The Church of England Records Centre

15 Galleywall Road, South Bermondsey, London, SE16 3PB.
Tel: 020 7898 1030;   Fax: 020 7898 7018;   Email: archivist@c-of-e.org.uk

The Conference of Religious

The General Secretary, PO Box 37602, The Ridgeway, London NW7 4XG.
Tel: 020 8201 1861;   Email: confrelig@aol.com
Website: www.corew.org

Copyright

Christian Copyright Licensing (Europe) Ltd [CCLI], PO Box 1339, Eastbourne, East Sussex BN21 1AD.
Tel: 01323 417711;   Email: info@ccli.co.uk   Website: www.ccli.co.uk

or

Calamus, Oak House, 70 High Street, Brandon, Suffolk, IP27 0AU.
Tel: 01842 819830;   Fax: 01842 819832

Criminal Records Bureau (CRB)

Customer Services, CRB, PO Box 110, Liverpool, L3 6ZZ.
Information Line: Tel: 0870 90 90 811;   Website: www.crb.gov.uk

Data Protection

Information Line: Tel: 01625 545745
Website: www.dataprotection.gov.uk

The Health and Safety Executive (HSE)

Information Service, Caerphilly Business Park, Caerphilly, CF83 3GG.
Information Line: Tel: 08701 545500
Website: www.hse.gov.uk

HSE Books, PO Box 1999, Sudbury, Suffolk, CO10 2WA.
Tel: 01787 881165
Website: www.hse.gov.uk/pubns

House of Bishops

Secretary to the House of Bishops, Central Secretariat, Church House, Great
Smith Street, London SW1P 3NZ.
Tel: 020 7898 1373

Lambeth Palace Library and Archives

Lambeth Palace Road, London, SE1 7JU.
Tel: 020 7898 1400;   Fax: 020 7928 7932
Website: www.lambethpalacelibrary.org

The Royal Commission on Historical Manuscripts

Quality House, Quality Court, Chancery Lane, London WC2 1HP.
Tel: 020 7242 1198;   Fax: 020 7831 3550
Website: www.hmc.gov.uk

VISITATION QUESTIONNAIRE

1)   Are there any significant changes in your life since the last Visitation of which you are aware? How has life in community affected you physically and emotionally? Have there been areas of strain that have had an adverse effect on your overall well-being?

2)   What nourishes your life at this stage? Do you find it generally possible to maintain a spirit of inner peace in the midst of the demands of life?

3)   Has there been provision for sufficient mental stimulation? What courses or training have you undertaken since the last Visitation? Have you found them helpful and creative?

4)   Have you been able to make good use of leisure activities of a relaxing and creative nature? Do you take your holidays?

5)   Are you happy with the quality of life in the community or do you find yourself often thinking and speaking negatively? Do you feel you are receiving adequate guidance, support and pastoral care?

6)   Do you feel your life and the community's are guided by Gospel values? Is the community following the spirit of the founder/foundress? What do you consider the value of the Religious Life for today's world?

7)   Do you feel comfortable with the Rule and related documents? Are Chapter meetings conducive to free expression?

8)   Is your work and ministry fulfilling? Do you see it as promoting or at least undergirding the mission/ministry of the community?

9)   Are there any areas of difficulty, e.g. relationships, work, authority, environment?

10) Do you feel fully involved in the life of the community? Is there any particular work to which you feel drawn? Along what lines would you see change and development and your part in this?

11) What difficulties, if any, do you experience in being present at the eucharist and Offices? Do you feel you have the right conditions for personal prayer, retreat days and annual retreat?

12) Have you any suggestions as to how the community's personal or corporate prayer life might be enriched or deepened?

13) Has community life made you more aware of your own particular strengths and weaknesses? If so, do you feel this has helped you grow or diminished you as a person? Are there ways in which the leadership could enable you to grow more?

14) Are there any personal concerns you wish to share?

SUGGESTIONS FOR A VISITATION QUESTIONNAIRE FOR THE LEADERSHIP TEAM

(If the community has other provinces or houses overseas they need to be appropriately included.)

1. What was the date of the last Visitation in this and the other provinces?
    (If there are other provinces or houses overseas, what are the arrangements regarding Visitations and what was the date when this happened last?)

Administration .

2. In the government or administration of the community, where action by the various Chapters or councils are required by the Statutes:
    (a)   has due notice of the agenda been given on all occasions?
    (b)   has a record of proceedings been kept?

3. Have all members of the various Chapters or councils had complete freedom in their deliberations?

4. How often do the different Chapters or councils meet?

5. Have such meetings of Chapters or councils as are prescribed by Statutes been duly held?

Noviciates and Houses

6. List the noviciate and branch houses (if applicable including those overseas) together with the names of the Religious residing in each.

7. What arrangements are made for the leader to visit the houses?

8. How is contact maintained with the different houses?

9. Have any houses overseas been closed or new ones opened since the last Visitation and has any new work been started or finished?

10. Are there any significant changes planned for the foreseeable future?

11. What are the arrangements concerning the Visitor and chaplains (including overseas houses)?

12. Where Religious are living singly, please give names and addresses.

13. What arrangements are made to meet the spiritual requirements of the life of each house?

14. Give details of the current warden/chaplain-general's term and how the office is fulfilled.

15. What provision is made for confessors and spiritual directors for members?

16. What is the provision made for sufficient time for private prayer, silence and solitude?

Financial and Legal

17. Are the auditors/ or independent examiners satisfied that the financial affairs of the community are satisfactory? If specific recommendations have been made have they been implemented?

18. List any other legal entities, charities, etc., related to the life, well-being and finances of the community.

19. Are all the community's members, staff, work and property adequately insured?

20. Have 'risk assessments' been completed on all relevant aspects of the community's life, related charities, work and properties?

21. What professional advice is available to you in regard to the community's investments?

22. Who provides the community with legal advice?

23. Have any official complaints been made against a member of the community? Has the complaints procedure been followed?

Fabric

24. Is the professional advice of an architect, surveyor or clerk of works available in regard to the property held by the community?

25. Is the fabric of the property(ies) deemed to be in a satisfactory condition? Are any substantial repairs or alterations needed, in either long or short term? If so, is the necessary money available?

26. Are there any substantial alterations of systems, fittings or appliances (e.g. heating or electrical equipment, etc.) necessary, involving considerable expense? Is the necessary money available?

Changes in Membership

27. Have any Religious been transferred since the last Visitation? If so please name them.
Has any transference been ratified by the Visitors of both communities concerned?
Please name any Religious who is in the process of exploring transference to this community.

28. Are any members of this community exploring transference to another community? If so what steps have been taken to ensure that the recipient community undertakes and is able to provide maintenance and spiritual provision as permanent as has been previously secured?

29. Have any members of the community been released and secularised since the last Visitation?

30. Are there any members who have absented themselves without permission and have refused to return when summoned? If so what action has been taken?

31. Have any members been secularised since the last Visitation?

Affiliated Persons

32. What name is used for this association? How many members are there? What is the relationship with the community?

The Life of the Community

Worship

33. Give a brief description of the community's life of common worship in the eucharist and the Office, listing the books used. Have there been any major changes since the last Visitation?

Ministry/Work

34. What are the main work commitments of members:
    (a) within each house;
    (b) outside the house they live in, paid or voluntary?

Study

35. What provision is made for members to read and study? In what way is this encouraged or guided?

36. Are members enabled to take further courses of study or training? How many have done so since the last Visitation?

Leisure

37. What annual provision is made for holidays?

38. How much time each week is there for creative leisure?

Health

39. Is medical assistance easily available? Who are the physicians to the community?

40. What are the arrangements regarding dentists?

41. What arrangements are made for those in need of nursing care?

42. Is professional psychiatric advice and help easily available? What is the number of members receiving therapy?

External

43. What is the relationship between the community and the local parishes?

44. What ecumenical contacts has the community had? Is there an exchange of Religious with the communities of other Churches?

45. How far are the community's members allowed or encouraged to become involved in social questions and those of peace and justice?

New members

46. What arrangements are made to check the medical and mental suitability of new members before acceptance?

47. What is the process the community uses to check possible new members with the Criminal Records Bureau?

48. What provision is made for the training of those testing their vocation?

49. Who has been received as a novice since the last Visitation?

50. Who has moved on to make vows/promises as a junior Religious since the last Visitation?

51. Who has been professed since the last Visitation?

52. Who has withdrawn from the community as a junior Religious since the last Visitation:
    (a) through their own initiative?
    (b) through the determination of the statutory authority of the community?

N.B. Please attach a full list of members of the community, their year of profession, the year of ordination if ordained, age and any professional qualifications (e.g. in teaching, social work, etc.).

GUIDELINES FOR THE ADMINISTRATION OF ARCHIVE COLLECTIONS

It is recommended that every community appoint an archivist, either from its members or from outside, to oversee the care, content and use of the collection. The archivist will need to have appropriate qualifications for the task or be encouraged to acquire such qualifications. The archivist's responsibilities for collecting material, and making it available for authorised use, should be clearly defined.

Therefore it is helpful in the first place for a job description to be drawn up. This will include terms of appointment, expected hours to be apportioned to this department and areas of confidentiality. Responsibilities in regard to museum items, photographs, audio-visual and machine-readable material should be set out. Volumes or documents pertaining to an archive collection include:

- Items relating to the founder or foundress: diaries, correspondence, personal biographical papers, portraits or photographs.
- Documents concerning the community's foundation (Constitution, Rule, provision of house, etc.)
- Legal papers relating to property occupied or owned by the community.
- Financial and administrative papers (items of historical significance, annual accounts, agreements with local authorities, and also illustrations of daily living).
- Papers relating to members (passed on from the superior's office) with consideration as to the appropriate confidentiality and possible period of closure.
- Memorabilia drawn from special occasions in the life of the community.

Agreement should be reached between the archivist and all officers of the community on the timing and method of transfer of non-current papers to the archive collection.

Ideally, appropriate provision should be made for the systematic storage of the archives, together with a realistic budget for the upkeep and administration of the records. A storage area should be allocated exclusively for the archives and the room made secure. Direct sunlight should be avoided and levels of temperature and humidity be kept even. A record should be kept of material removed from the collection and the photocopying of original documents can be a sensible means of providing required material without risking loss or unnecessary wear and tear.

Communities would normally wish to open their archives to those undertaking research. However, it is wise to draw up written rules concerning supervision and for access by visiting scholars and other researchers. These should include working arrangements, security, supervision, photography and photocopying, the lending of material, etc. The overall purpose for such work should also be established and where advisable it should be stated that nothing may be published without the permission of the superior. Terms of copyright should be established. Most record offices, including church organisations, open papers to the public after thirty years, or in the case of personal papers a hundred years. Papers should not be withheld from use without good cause.

(See Officers and Employees paragraph **911**; Communities and Ecclesiastical Authority paragraph **1003** & Closure paragraph **1308**).

THE CRIMINAL RECORDS BUREAU / DISCLOSURE

The Criminal Records Bureau (CRB) is an executive agency of the Home Office in Great Britain, set up in 2001 to assist organisations, including churches and communities, to establish the suitability of an individual for work or association with children or vulnerable adults.

The service aims to provide a comprehensive search, through police and other records, to ensure there is nothing in an individual's record that would render them unsuitable for employment or voluntary work, where such work includes association with children or other vulnerable people.

There is a requirement for all communities engaged in public service of this kind to negotiate a means of registration, either independently or by joining with another agency (e.g. the diocese). Having registered or become attached to a body registered with the CRB, an individual search may be initiated by means of the individual completing a Disclosure Application Form to which the CRB respond with an impartial and confidential document known as a 'Disclosure'. A copy of this Disclosure is sent in confidence to the community's named signatory. Various fees are payable.

The Disclosure also acts as a protection both for the individual and the community, who are left particularly vulnerable otherwise when working within these sensitive areas. CRB checks are no substitute for proper vigilance and good child protection practice.

See also paragraphs **203, 709, 914, 1008** and **Useful Addresses – CRB**

CHARITY LAW REGARDING THE PAYMENTS TO INDIVIDUALS

Under English civil law charities may only make payments to individuals in these ways:

- By charitable application: These are payments made within the stated objects of the charity.
- By contract: These are payments made in settlement of amounts owed by the charity, say for payments to employees or to suppliers of materials or services.
- By way of compensation, where ordered by a Court of law, or settled on professional advice to avoid a claim going to Court.
- By way of ex-gratia payment. Section 27 of the Charities Act 1993 states that the Trustees of the charity must ask the Charity Commission for consent in the case where it is intended that a payment be made by way of moral obligation.

(The above is based on advice given by Buzzacott, Chartered Accountants in their booklet, *Financial arrangements for a member leaving a Religious Order.*)

RELIGIOUS LIVING THE EREMITICAL LIFE

1   The life of complete solitude in prayer and silence before God is a continuing element of the Christian spiritual tradition. Although it involves external separation from society, it is a life lived in profound communion with the whole Church and with all humanity. Living in simplicity and poverty, the Religious is identified with all humanity in its need and poverty before God.

2   Vocation to the eremitical life is sometimes part of the developing vocation of a member of a Religious community. There is also an intermediate form in which a small community devoted to prayer and silence, often with individual dwelling places, bears many marks of the eremitical life without a complete withdrawal from all social intercourse.

A Religious who is aware of a strong call to the eremitical way of life requires experienced guidance during a lengthy period of preparation before the matter is laid before the community for implementation. There must be close collaboration between the spiritual director, the superior and the Visitor. The bishop of the place where the Religious is to live should be informed.

A period for testing this vocation may be provided in a place near the buildings of the community; or in a settlement of hermits; or, if all those involved in guidance are agreed, in a place of greater physical isolation.

The Religious remains a member of the community in which vows have been professed, even though the eremitical life has distinctive characteristics, demands and obligations.

The Chapter must give approval before a member undertakes this way of life. Once this life has been undertaken, the Chapter government of the community will have no direct relevance to the life of the hermit, who will be under the personal direction either of the superior of the community or some other experienced person agreed by the superior and the Religious, and approved by the Chapter. During the period of probation, the Religious will relinquish Chapter rights.

If the period of probation proves that there is no permanent vocation to solitude, the Religious should return without question to the place formerly held in the community.

If the vocation proves permanent, it should eventually be given formal recognition by the Chapter. This recognition would imply final relinquishment of Chapter rights on the part of the member, and acknowledgement of the permanence of the eremitical vocation by the community. The community will retain concern for the spiritual and physical well-being of the hermit, especially in old age.

3   Communities should bear in mind that many Religious feel the need for shorter or longer periods of solitude in which they may give themselves more completely to silence and prayer. This natural need may have to be distinguished from an eremitical vocation in particular cases. Some communities will provide suitable accommodation for such periods of withdrawal, or permit some of their members to spend periods sharing in the life of a monastic community where normally more silence and solitude are part of the life.

4   Those concerned with the administration of communities must be prepared to distinguish clearly between a true vocation to the eremitical life and the temptation of some Religious to seek this way of life as a way of avoiding the obligations of obedience and the demands of the common life. In general it will be found that the possessor of a true eremitical vocation will be characterised by humility and will be undemanding, a good community member without marked foibles, but with a genuine attraction to silence.

A Note on the Spiritual Direction of Hermits

5   The Religious who is able to undertake a life of prayer in solitude will be one who already has a stable relationship with God in prayer and is simple and uncomplicated in relating to other people and in the material concerns of life. This disposition of unwavering trust in God, and in God's providence through those who minister to their basic spiritual and material needs, is necessary for sustaining a spirit of solitude and inner silence. The spiritual director, though not themselves living the life, should be of a similar disposition. The hermit and the director need to be able to recognise each other as kindred spirits in this respect.

Since the hermit's rhythm of life and mode of prayer should be created out of their direct dependence upon, and co-operation with, the Holy Spirit, and will be unique to that person, the director should not interfere with that formation, nor normally initiate changes. However, the director should be sufficiently knowledgeable concerning the Church's tradition of spiritual growth and of the eremitical life in particular as to be able to detect deviations from the way. In monitoring the hermit's life from the point of view of its goal – union with God through Jesus Christ – the director should be available to encourage, to confirm developments, to warn of temptations, to keep trials in proportion, and always as a fellow pilgrim to point the way to God.

Frequent meeting is not desirable, and most questions might be dealt with by correspondence. Above all, the director must maintain detachment, so as to be able to identify with the hermit in prayer and counsel without imposing self-generated patterns or solutions to problems arising. There must be a mutual listening for the leading of the Holy Spirit. If not a priest, or not living at a convenient distance from the hermit, the director may suitably arrange for another sympathetic priest to celebrate the eucharist occasionally in the hermit's dwelling-place and (with the permission of the Ordinary of the place) reserve the Blessed Sacrament for regular holy communion.

The director needs to remember that it is the superior of the hermit's community who makes provision for their accommodation, decides with the member how community observances such as the Divine Office or enclosure are to be adapted for their life, provides for their maintenance, and is responsible for decisions about health care, and when they have become too infirm to live in solitude. In all such matters the task of the director is to help the hermit make the best use of what is provided or decided.

SOLITARIES WHO ARE NOT MEMBERS OF A RELIGIOUS COMMUNITY

(a) Men and women, who are free of family or other prior responsibilities, can follow a calling to a solitary life without receiving any formal ecclesiastical recognition or title. Any person so called will need the direction of an experienced spiritual guide both in the testing and living out of this vocation. Much of what is said concerning the direction of hermits (Appendix VI, 5) can be applied also to solitaries who are Religious. If they live in the simplicity of poverty, the dedication of chastity, and under the guidance of an experienced spiritual director, such a vocation is self-authenticating.

(b) There needs to be an adequate period of time for testing the vocation before undertaking a vow of celibacy where there is a calling to do so (see Appendix VIII on the Public Making of Personal Vows).

(c) Such a solitary will probably choose a simple form of dress; but the wearing of a habit which implies membership of a Religious community is inappropriate. For the same reason it is not desirable that a Religious name or title should be adopted.

Simply as solitaries devoted to a life of prayer they do not come into the formal category of Religious, since the latter are members of a Religious community accepted as such by the authority of the Church. For the purposes of this *Handbook* in regard to the solitary life, the term hermit refers to a member of a Religious Community and the term solitary refers to one who is not a Religious.

THE PUBLIC MAKING OF PERSONAL VOWS

1 There have always been some who believe that they are called by God to dedicate themselves by a vow and to live as consecrated celibates, whose primary concern is to build up the body of Christ in unity and love, though without living a common life under a superior and a common Rule. This autonomous vowed life has been recognised in the Eastern and Western Churches from earliest times as an authentic Christian vocation. Because it is not a life lived in community according to the norms of the Religious Life, it does not come within the normal scope of the Advisory Council; but since it has some similarities to the situation of Religious living under vows, bishops and others have frequently referred cases to the Council. Therefore the Council has set up a Personal Vows Advisory Group to which these requests are to be referred. Their paper and Guidelines are to be found on page 74 of this *Handbook*.

2 The Council offers the following guidelines:

(a) The whole-hearted commitment, dedication and offering of any Christian to God is to be encouraged and supported by the Church. However, the desire of anyone to make the commitment publicly by pronouncing a vow of celibacy needs to be examined and discerned carefully and wisely. A person believing they are called to do so should discuss this with their parish priest and their spiritual director, and with their support approach the diocesan bishop. The bishop, who alone has authority to receive such a public commitment by vow, is strongly advised to avail themselves of the further guidance and support of the Personal Vows Advisory Group set up by the Advisory Council for testing these vocations, which can also provide a service for making and blessing the vow.

(b) It is unlikely that people living alone within the context of, say, a parish community could undertake the other traditional vows of poverty and obedience, since these vows would imply shared ownership of resources and communally ordered decision-making for the sake of the kingdom. Therefore normally only the vow of celibacy should be undertaken.

(c) The wearing of a habit similar to that worn by members of a Religious community is inappropriate, since those who make a vow outside of a Religious community are not included in the formal category of Religious. For the same reason it is not desirable that a Religious name or title be adopted.

(d) In receiving this vow, the bishop should make it clear that they or their successors are not responsible for providing work, an income, or accommodation. As chief pastor of the diocese, they take spiritual responsibility for the person under vow, though they would normally delegate this to a designated priest of experience.

(e) Should the person under vow move into another diocese, the bishop who has previously acted as guardian of the vow should commend that person to the care of the bishop of the receiving diocese. Likewise, a retiring bishop should commend any such under their care to their successor.

(f) The bishop should register with the Administrative Secretary of the Advisory Council the names of all those who make this vow in public.

(g) The dispensing authority for this vow is the bishop who is currently the guardian of the vow.

PERSONAL VOWS
for those living the single consecrated life

The Background

The Bible commends chastity lived out in life-long marriage or celibacy as ways of living the Christian life. From earliest times, inspired by the Holy Spirit, some have followed the call of God to live their vocation in a covenant relationship of consecrated celibacy. Throughout history this *charism* has taken a variety of forms. In the early Church, the place of consecrated virgins and widows was honoured.[1] Tertullian was the first to equate such a vocation with marriage so that consecration to celibacy was seen as a spiritual espousal.[2] The monastic life developed in Syria and Egypt with its eremitic and coenobitic traditions incorporating celibacy. From this developed the celibate Religious Life in its various Western expressions. The rules of cloistered enclosure were introduced in the thirteenth century at a time when the mendicant preaching orders were being established. The Middle Ages witnessed the Beguine movement in the Low Countries and consecrated tertiaries living in the world like St Catherine of Siena and St Rose of Lima. In the seventeenth century, Mary Ward and St Vincent de Paul established new forms of the Religious Life.

Celtic monasticism and anchorites were a particular British expression of the Religious Life. Today in Britain and elsewhere we see new forms of the consecrated life emerging – among them secular institutes, dispersed communities, the Order of Consecrated Virgins in the Roman Catholic Church and a growth in those seeking to live as hermits and solitaries. Alongside these are men and women who wish to consecrate their lives in celibacy to live as single people in the world for the sake of the kingdom of God.

Celibacy as a *charism*

At times in the history of the Church, celibacy has been elevated as a superior vocation, but in a post-modern society it is often regarded as irrelevant and life-denying. For some, it has been sought as a refuge from sexuality, commitment and intimacy, or it is regarded as the fate of the sad, the unlucky and the ugly! There is a need to reinterpret and renew this biblical vocation and for the Church to support and encourage those who are called to this way of life.

---

[1] 'Their ranks were recruited from both sexes, even at an early period; we note their presence even in the second century under various names, such as *ascetae, eunuchs, continentes, encratitae etc'*. L. Duchesne in *Christian Worship*, SPCK, London, 1912 p.419f.

[2] 'What makes the virgin the 'spouse' or 'bride of Christ' is not the fact of her vow of virginity, but rather her relationship with Christ, which includes and demands virginity. To speak of a woman as 'virgin' is to speak of this profound relationship rather than to speak of a physical state.' Teresa Clements DMJ in *Order of the Consecration of Virgins*, Milltown Studies, 1989.

Celibacy is an invitation, a gift and a means of grace. Those who seek to make a vow of celibacy, usually through a bishop, do so in a way similar to that which others choose when they make a vow of marriage. It is a loving response to a God who invites someone to consecrate his or her sexuality in this way. It is a distinctive *charism* and is incarnational; it is a counter-cultural witness in a world obsessed with sex and binds the vowed person to Christ to serve him with a new freedom. Those who respond to this invitation discover that God does indeed bless them. They are more available to others and they have an inner solitude that can foster prayer, but they also learn that like their married friends, they need to renew their vow every day.

For some, celibacy is a secondary vocation which may develop into a charism, but is freely accepted as part of another vocation – for example, a commitment to serve the poor, missionary service, a dedication to widowhood, membership of a Religious community or the Roman Catholic priesthood.

For others, celibacy is a primary vocation. It is indeed like a 'spiritual marriage' and they feel 'complete' through their consecration of celibacy. Here there is also an eschatological dimension, for in heaven 'they neither marry nor are given in marriage' *(Mark 12:25)*.

From Apostolic times, God has called people to consecrated celibacy. Today, we need to respond positively to those who are being called and to make the Church aware of this gift and way of life. We need to support and encourage those who seek to live out this consecration in the world in response to God's invitation to follow the way of Christ.

Personal Vow(s)
These are promises made to a bishop (or his delegate) by an individual who is not a member of a Religious community for a temporary period or for life. They are better not described as private vows because they are being officially received and recognised and of course, all vows are 'personal' in that they are made by a person to God. The term personal vow is therefore preferred to private or individual vow.

Consecrated celibacy
The personal vow will be that of 'consecrated celibacy', which is the touchstone of the Religious Life. The vow both recognises the 'call' of the person making it, and the gift the person has received and now offers back to God and the Church for the sake of the kingdom.

The single consecrated life

Those living the single consecrated life are distinguished from hermits who are professed Religious vowed to the evangelical counsels or the Benedictine Rule. Some who choose the single consecrated life will be called to an active apostolate and others to a mixed or contemplative spiritual life.

Guidelines

A vocation to the single consecrated life should be tested over a period of time before temporary vows are made.

The candidate should have a spiritual director who is familiar with this form of consecration.

A proper enquiry should be made of the candidate – and the attached questionnaire indicates the areas of enquiry.

The vocation is rooted in God – it is about 'being' rather than 'doing' – but the vocation also needs to be rooted in the Church by association with a parish, chaplaincy or Religious community.

After a period of probation, annual temporary vows may be received, and renewed, using a form of service that recognises the maturity, perseverance and significance of the consecration being made and renewed.

The length of time in temporary vows will depend on each particular candidate, but life vows should only be made with the support of those who have been involved in the discernment process. Temporary vows may be renewed and thirty should be regarded as the minimum age for making a life vow.

Candidates should be single, widowed or divorced. Someone who is still bound to marriage vows may not take a vow of celibacy.

A ring and/or a cross may be appropriate symbols of the covenant relationship being undertaken.

A personal vow should be received by a bishop who will keep a record of it and also inform the Advisory Council and the diocesan bishop if another bishop has received the vow. The bishop of the diocese in which a vowed person lives shall also have authority to grant release from the vow, at which point the Advisory Council should again be notified.

If a vowed person moves to another diocese, the bishop should commend the person to the bishop of the diocese to which the person is moving.

An annual meeting with the bishop (either personally or through a delegate) is advised. He should also ensure that a vowed person has an adequate network of spiritual support and the means to maintain a lifestyle suitable to his/her vocation.

A candidate may take an additional vow(s) in addition to consecrated celibacy to indicate a lifestyle (for example, simplicity, hospitality, commitment to the poor) or a particular devotion (for example, to the Blessed Sacrament, intercession, etc.). Although candidates will be expected to live within the spirit of the evangelical counsels, it is not appropriate to take vows of poverty and obedience as the candidate retains control of personal finances and has no Religious superior.

It will help if aspirants and single consecrated people can be put in touch with others who have taken a similar vow either within the Church of England or with a member of the Order of Consecrated Virgins (OCV) within the Roman Catholic Church.

In due course, we trust that there will be an increasing number who will form a network to support one another. Key ingredients in this support will be encouragement in the distinctiveness and variety of the call on each person's life and the recognition that this will continue to grow and change over time.

Personal encouragement and formal recognition by a bishop can be an important factor in developing individual vocations. At this point in time bishops have a particular opportunity to promote this step as both an ancient and contemporary expression of the consecrated life offering enrichment to the Church today.

ENQUIRY FOR BISHOPS RECEIVING PERSONAL VOWS OF SINGLE CONSECRATED PERSONS

1. **Personal details:** Name, address, telephone number, email, date of birth etc.

2. **Personal circumstances:** Education, occupation, financial circumstances, housing, pension, family, daily pattern of life, etc. Single, widowed or divorced?

3. **Faith journey:** Write about your faith journey and other significant events and influences in your life. How does your faith relate to the whole of your life (e.g. family friendships, work)?

4. **Spiritual Life:** Spiritual director? Confessor? Link with a Religious community? Theological study and spiritual reading. Have you always been single?

5. **Formation:** Are you in contact with a single consecrated person? If not, would you be willing to be put in touch with one?

6. **Pattern of Prayer:** When do you attend the eucharist, Offices, spend time in personal prayer, retreat?

7. **Parish involvement:** How do you participate and contribute to the life of the parish? How would you see consecrated celibacy as contributing to your life in the church?

8. **Work & Ministry:** Have you been involved in a recognised ministry within the Church? If so, please provide details.

9. **Health:** Health history? Disabilities? Have you received psychiatric care or counselling? Are you willing to undergo a medical examination/psychological assessment?

10. **Consecration:** How did you learn about the single consecrated life. Write about why you wish to be consecrated. If you are consecrated, how do you see that as affecting your future?

11. **References:** Please provide the names of two referees (e.g. parish priest, spiritual director).

INDEX

'acknowledged' community 2–3

Advisory Council (ACRBRC)
> address 69; and closure of communities 61, 62; Constitution of v; and the Directory/ Handbook i; and exclaustration 19; history of vi–viii; and new communities 59, 60; and personal vows 87; and property 41; registers held by 3, 88; and Visitors 51, 52; and wardens 47

appeals 52

Archbishop of Canterbury 23, 25

archives 63, 79–80

archivist 49, 79

aspirants 4–5, 35

associates 37, 38–9

Benedictines 2, 10, 38, 46

Bursar 49

Canon Law 32, 53

Central Board of Finance of the Church of England Funds 42

chaplain-general 34–5, 47–8, 62, 67

chaplains 35, 48, 62

Chapter 27–30

Charity Commissioners 40, 45, 57, 70

charity law 13, 40, 41, 48, 52, 62, 63, 82

children/minors 5, 6, 53

closure of a community 37, 41, 47, 52, 61–4

clothing 7

community obligations 33

communities
> and common terminology 32; contact between 1, 5; new 59–60; and transference 18–19

complaints 67

confessor extraordinary 35

confessors 48

conscience 11

Constitution
> and admission and training 6, 7; alteration and suspension 37; and Chapter 27, 28, 29, 30; and the Church 1; and closure 41, 61, 62, 63; and community definition 2; definition 31–2; and detached service 17; and exclaustration 1; and ex-members 23; and leave of absence 17; and officers 46, 47, 48; and profession and vows 9, 12, 13; and property

94

as 'ordinary' 2, 52–3; and postulants 6; and property 13, 43; and spiritual directors 48–9; and transference 15